Paintings and Musings from the Heartland

Paintings and Musings from the Heartland

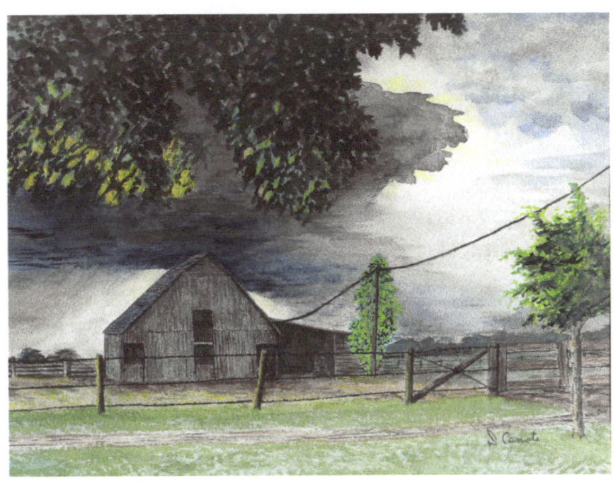

Dorothy Canote

Compass Flower Press
Columbia, Missouri

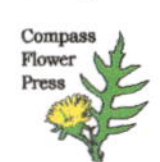

Published by Compass Flower Press
Columbia, MO 65203

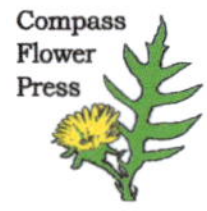

Library of Congress Control Number: 2020900147
ISBN: 978-1-942168-97-3

Cover painting: Barn on Montague Hill, Marshall, Missouri

This barn sits on what was formerly the England farm, owned by the family of my first husband. It is located east of Marshall, Missouri, off State Highway 41, the elevated location known as Montague Hill, no doubt for an original settler. The hovering storm clouds are symbolic of storms that pass through all our lives.

Dedication

This collection of paintings and musings is dedicated to Gladys Swan, whose urging prompted me to do something I always wanted to do—write.

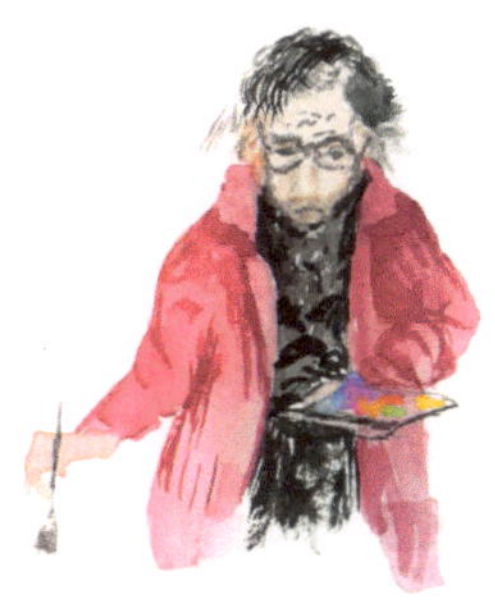

Gladys Swan

Table of Contents

Introduction

In The Beginning

The Columbia Art Group

It's been a few years now since Cynthia Durost, a wonderful lady and talented artist, began teaching watercolor classes at Columbia's National Guard Armory. Classes were initially offered through Columbia Parks and Recreation, and we spent a couple of years learning the basics before the classes were discontinued. We were having so much fun we started getting together once a week at different homes to splash watercolor on paper and continue our friendship. Our ever-evolving group of painters has stabilized at about ten to twelve dedicated and lovely women who still meet weekly to create expressions of our artistic talents, and to attempt to solve some of the world's problems.

When our group began, we were all pretty much on the same blank piece of paper, so to speak. Over the first years, we explored and found our way through washes, dabs, trying out different brushes, paints, paper, and so forth. With practice we began to find our own styles, techniques, and our favorite subjects. On any given day you might see wildlife and wildflowers, abstract designs, scenes of countrysides, towns, seashores, and still life subjects on our papers.

My Painting Odyssey

After several years of meeting nearly every Tuesday, I began to amass a considerable cache of paintings. I began to explore the local farmers market as a sales opportunity for them alongside my produce, herbs, and cut flowers. It turned out there were enough people out there who appreciated my modest efforts and who had bare spots on their walls, desks, niches, and other spaces who were willing to give a home to my paintings.

Still the works accumulate, and this year, having hung a bunch of them up in my booth at Columbia's Earth Day event, several of my friends and fellow painters dropped by to give me some much appreciated support. A member of our group, Gladys Swan, suggested I might consider collecting some of them into a book, accompanied by a narrative of what I found interesting enough about the subject to paint it. Gladys is herself an accomplished artist and author, and I thought, *why not?* Something else to keep me off the streets and out of trouble.

So I began, and since Gladys started it all, I asked her to critique my first efforts. She wanted more; she urged me to allow the reader to understand what compelled me to paint the scenes I chose, what they meant to me personally—as a means to reveal some of the story of my life.

Finding Subjects to Paint

I find that I gravitate toward realism, and enjoy trying to render the detail of a scene. The challenge of capturing the roughness of tree bark, the shapes and shadows of leaves and stones, and the color variations of skies and clouds gives me great satisfaction—when I'm successful.

At some point I discovered bridges. And old buildings. Wow! Those were fun! I spent weeks digging out books from the library and online to learn more about bridges, how they are built, what they're made of, and the history of how they have evolved. I finally painted my way through pretty much every type of historic bridge, including the various materials and designs. The only problem is that not many people want to fill up their walls with twelve by fourteen paintings of bridges, no matter how good they are. (I'm still looking for a bridge engineer who wants them all!)

When I found some old black and white photos of houses, barns, schools, and churches that offered some interesting possibilities, I tackled those for a while, and began to become interested in the historical aspects of the subject matter. By now, you may have figured out that I have a tendency to become distracted by my subjects, and to wander off down figurative pathways investigating . . . whatever. Yep, you're so right.

So whether or not you appreciate or agree with my rationalizations, if you care to browse my somewhat abridged library of offerings and personal reflections, I can only thank you for taking the time, and hope you enjoy the journey.

Chapter 1
Scenes from My Home Grounds

Our childhoods are not all the same, obviously, but each has a significant role in leading us to who we become as adults. Growing up in my small town in a rural community in northern Missouri was, at least for me, about as idyllic as it could get. The components of such a community (if it is stable and complete and if the town is more than just a wide spot in the road) have some commonalities. These may include a public school system, one or more churches, a grocery store or two, a gas station, cafe, and perhaps some sort of club, fraternal organization, or other such institution that draws people together. Also, depending on the makeup of its citizens, perhaps in inverse proportion to the number of churches, there may be a bar or pool hall.

Then, as now, rural communities exist in a matrix of surrounding towns and the countryside around and between them. Their proximity fosters both social interactions and competitions among and between schools and clubs, as well as economic interests. County fairs, 4-H clubs, church bazaars, and—in our part of the county, 'coon hunts—were all great venues that tied together the fabric of our otherwise separate and divergent lives.

In the course of researching some of the subjects I painted, I learned quite a lot about my hometown and the adjacent area. In retrospect, I also experienced a growing awareness of what should have been obvious; that the cultural and genetic makeup of a town and its surroundings reflect the origin and culture of its founding settlers. Missouri is no different in that respect than any other state, so it is common to find entire communities with a specific ethnic origin.

As time passes, children grow up and marry, have children and then grandchildren, the community genes intermingle, recombine and disperse. The makeup of the population changes with the influx of newcomers and egress of residents seeking other venues or economic opportunities.

At the same time, as houses, buildings, roads and utilities deteriorate or are abandoned due to lack of use, other such infrastructure is added, remodeled, and generally improved. But old buildings, bridges, and scenes, lacking evidence of improvements, hold an interest and charm for me that leads me to paint them before they are lost to history. Indeed, some such subjects have already been lost, and remain only as photographs in books and archives.

Painting these old scenes is my homage to the subject. I experience the reality of the subject, which in turn evokes a memory of those who also experienced its place in the history of the town, the community, and their lives.

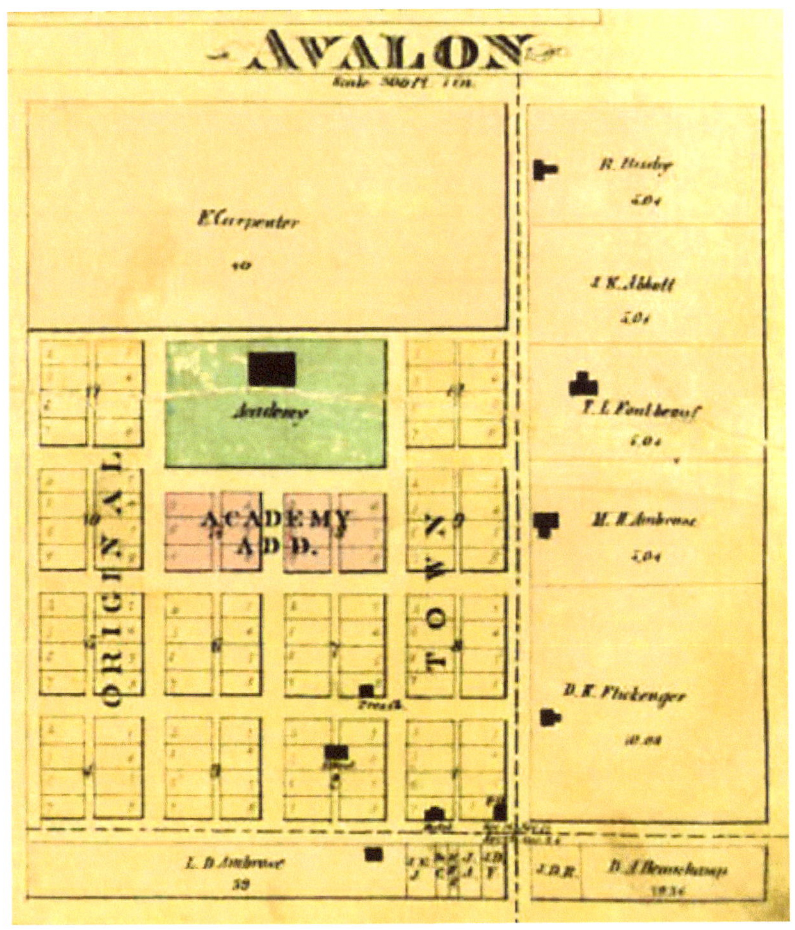

Painting Avalon—Main Street

Avalon, Missouri, population varying somewhere between fifty and one hundred, depending on the year and population of dogs (popular joke). "My home town..." she says with affection. In my home town every street, gravel and dirt road—or mud, depending on the season—was as familiar to me as the rooms in our house. As was the case in most small towns then, everywhere was safe and neighbors were always nearby to keep an eye on the relatively small population of barefoot children who migrated from one house to the next. We couldn't get away with anything without someone seeing and reporting, darn it!

The town was laid out by David Carpenter in 1869 in a grid of sixteen blocks in a four by four arrangement. Each block had eight lots, with a fair proportion of residents owning two lots, or even four for the more affluent. One entire block (number 2 on map at left) was devoted to the school, and four blocks were originally owned by the Avalon Academy, a college of sorts. While most streets were the modest width of two cars, Main Street was wide enough to accommodate side parking, a center row of parallel parking, and one lane on either side, up and down the street.

Our house was less than a block away from Main Street and I could hardly wait to get up on the morning after Halloween. Main Street sometimes had implements, outhouses, or evidence of other mischief perpetrated by the local teenage hooligans. It was almost as exciting as Christmas morning!

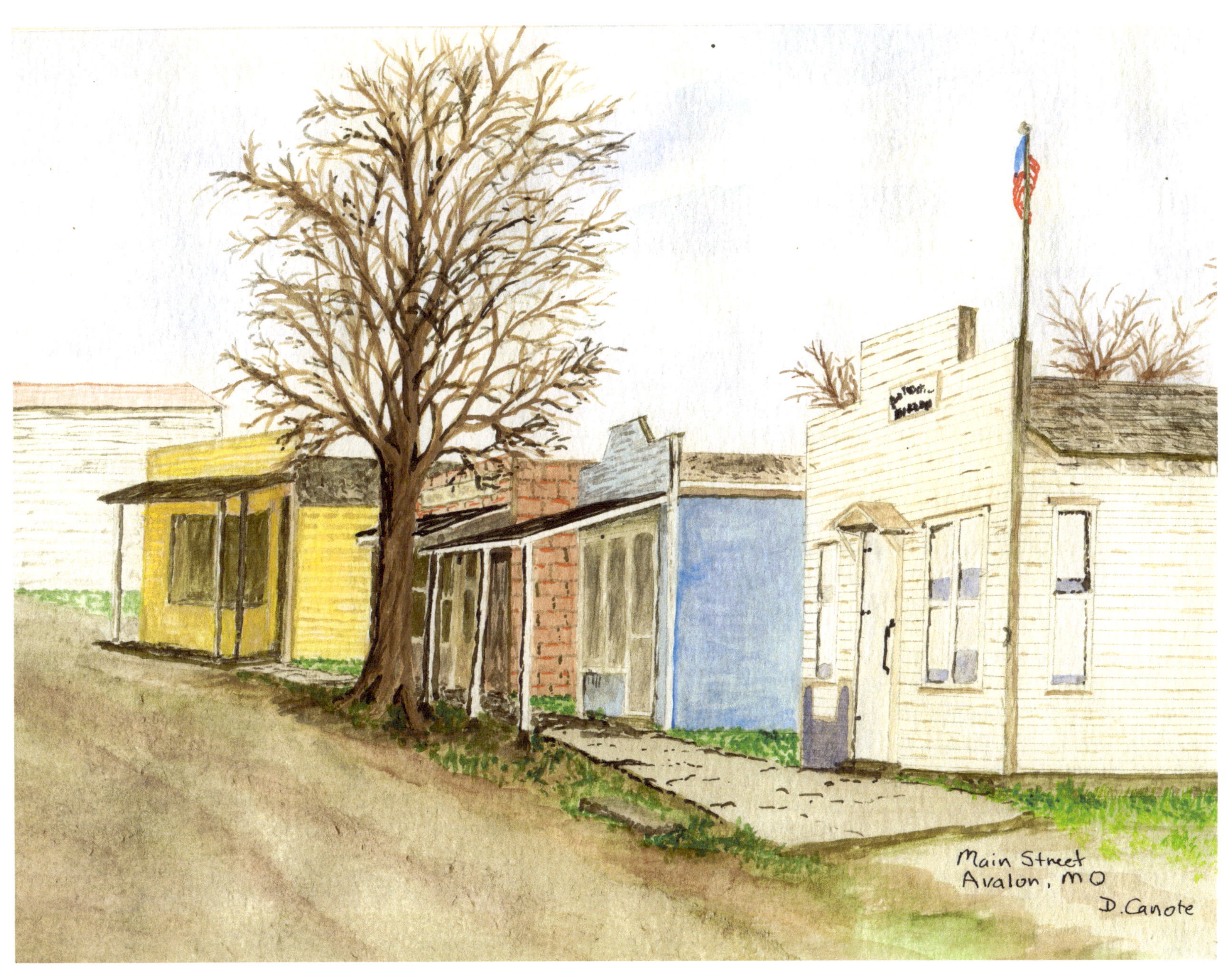
Main Street
Avalon, MO
D. Canote

My mother, then the town's postmaster (formerly always the masculine, regardless of gender), often made me the unofficial letter carrier for the old residents who had no means of transportation and were unable to walk even the few blocks from their homes. Using my bike, I was also the meals on wheels for those same old folks, so I knew most of Avalon's population pretty well.

In addition to the U.S. Post Office (white building with the flag), Main Street was at one time also fronted by a hotel (burned down), a bank (gold brick—*ha, ha*—far left), a barbershop (blue), a feed store (red brick), and, to the right of the post office, a large building that housed a grocery, meat locker and pool hall—which I had strict instructions to stay out of. That was kind of hard, since the hand-dipped ice cream freezer was just inside the connecting door to the grocery. Above the pool hall was a 'dance hall' which I never saw, but which my brother Jerry frequented late at night for weekly poker games. Reports had it that at any given time there might be several thousand dollars on the table. I always wondered about how some of those guys could afford those new cars . . . .

Within a block of Main Street was the IOOF Lodge (Independent Order of Odd Fellows), the Methodist church, Fink's store (dry goods and nickel candy), Avery's store (liver sausage), a tiny gas station, and the telephone exchange. One accessed the operator by turning the crank on the side of the phone box. (Nellie . . . don't listen in!) Nearly all the homes were on party lines, so you had to listen for the number of long and short rings to identify yours, and if it wasn't, you could secretly listen. That was how a lot of news got around. "Oh, I thought that was my ring." I believe it was some time in the sixties, while I was off at college, when Avalon got around to putting in private lines, after which folks had to join a church or the PTA to find out the gossip.

Between the empty bank and the feed store—officially referred to as "the exchange building" (what did one exchange?) was a vacant lot that in the summer would provide a space for outdoor movies. I was allowed to attend some of these, when the 'Mom rating scale' determined that the subject matter was fit for a child's viewing. I did manage to get into one, a western, that was a bit more bloody than I was really ready for. Some years the school grounds, across the street from the Post Office, would host a tent revival—a huge nondenominational draw, with all the attendant hymn singing and hallelujahs and plenty of souls saved. Temporarily.

The large maple tree in front of the barbershop is still there, larger than ever and intent on pushing up the sidewalk in front of the buildings. The buildings in my paintings are also extant, with the exception of the bank, later demolished and now the parking lot of a bar and grill, which serves as the town's social center and the location of our annual Memorial Day Avalon Reunion.

This sampling of my memories is probably similar to those of many other souls who were fortunate enough to grow up in a farming community's small town. Those years all seem to meld together like the ingredients of a cake, so it is hard to recall exactly in what years and in what sequence events occurred. It was a great place for a child to grow up, and for folks to grow old.

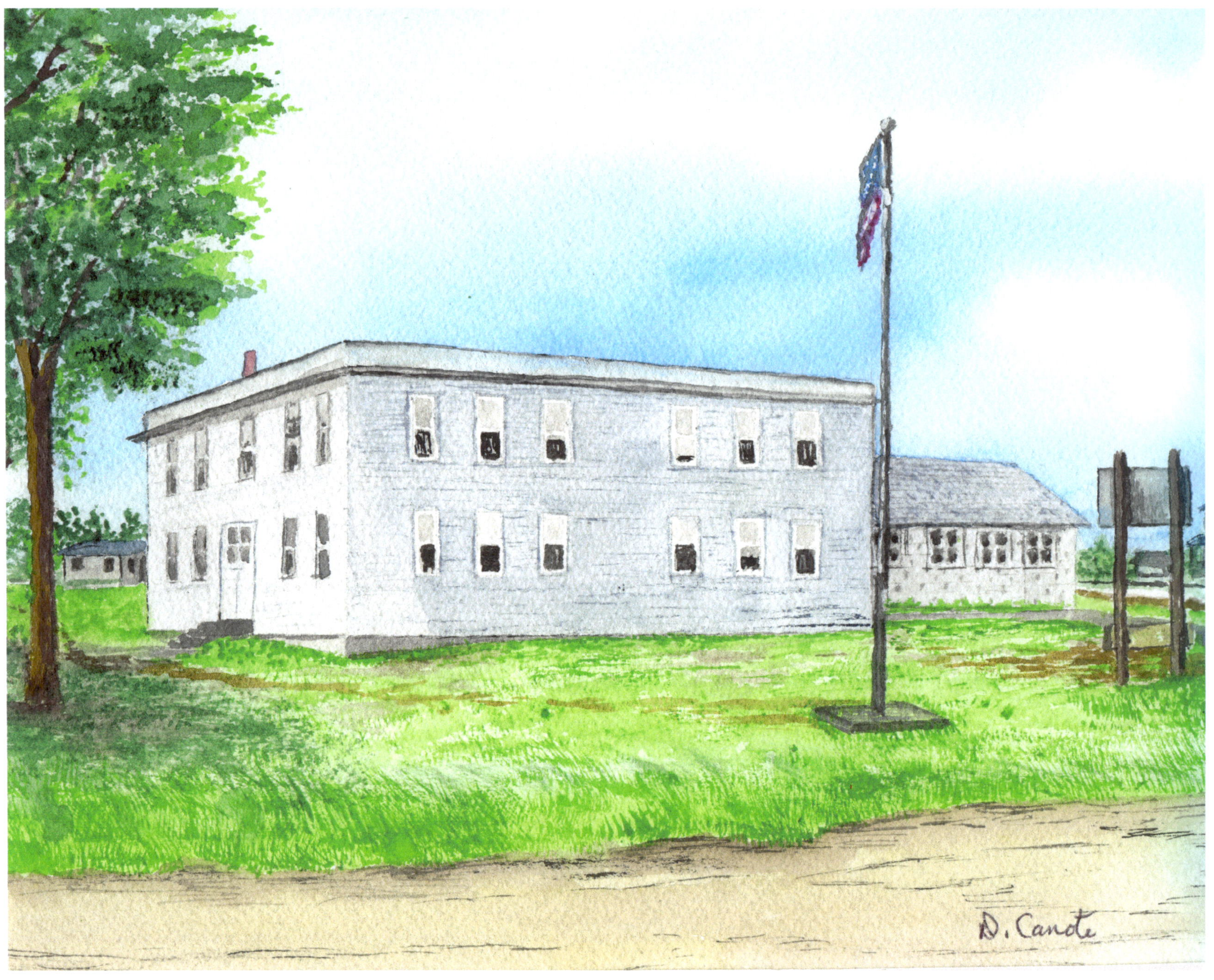
D. Canote

Avalon School

An 1853 Act of the Missouri General Assembly provided the structure for a uniform school system throughout the state. This act authorized the Livingston County School Commission, beginning in 1865, to appoint a county superintendent to license teachers. A copy of the abstract for the school grounds indicated that the town's founder, David Carpenter, sold the entire block to the Livingston County school district in 1870, so the school itself was probably built soon after that date.

Avalon's first school would have been referred to as a 'village' school, and was initially one story, containing grades one through eight. A second story was added at a later date which provided space for high school classrooms. When I attended there for my first three years of grade school, a cafeteria had been added on the north side of the main building. This section was retained when the remainder of the school was demolished in 1956, and remodeled into a home, which still stands.

The first floor on the east side was divided into two large classrooms, one for grades one through three and the other for grades four through six, with one teacher for each classroom. The entire west side downstairs served as the auditorium and gymnasium, with a stage for music classes, programs, and performances. On rainy days it was used for that diversion so essential to the sanity of both students and teachers—recess. Otherwise, it was, "Outdoors with you!" This glorious activity consisted of fifteen to thirty minutes mid-morning, after lunch, and mid-afternoon of largely unsupervised (as I remember it) mayhem and games, swings, and teasing by the boys.

Upstairs, which I don't recall ever seeing, were the high school classrooms. However, I know there was at least one room for business classes, thanks to my brother Jerry, who was always full of stories of his teenage exploits. He recounted at one point an incident about himself and another ne'er-do-well pal sneaking into the business classroom one day and removing all the little screws that stopped the carriage returns on the old typewriters. Then they lurked outside below the windows, waiting to hear the little *ding*s that notified the typist at the end of a line of type. This was followed within a few seconds by the sound of the unfettered carriages hitting the blackboard to the left of the outer row of tables, while a few of them flew out the open upstairs windows and landed on the lawn. Jerry never did say what the punishment was for the prank, but like most of the mischief that occurred, the principal knew who to blame, calling out the door, "Deardorff! Dowell! Get in here!"

Since most of my memories of those three years have been erased by time, there are only a few things to add. In most photos of the building there are some important things missing. To the south was the path to the set of heavy-duty swings and monkey bar, with a huge slide, whose use was preempted by the first kids out the door at recess. Claiming a swing was followed by the process of standing and pumping up until the swing was level with the bars (top cross bar), followed by bailing out. Wonder of wonders, no bones were ever broken that I know of, and the thrill of letting go and dropping through the air probably gave me the nerve to step off the ledge the first time I went rappelling later in life.

Two paths to the west were, as you might guess, to the Boys' and Girls' outhouses. A favorite pastime of the boys was to hang out behind the Girls' and torment the users inside by banging with sticks on the brick wall. Enough said about that.

The flag pole to the east, across from the post office, was added sometime in the early 1950s. A final memory of the old school is evidenced by a scrapbook photo that my mother took with her ubiquitous Brownie camera, of me about age seven on the south steps after winning best costume at the school Halloween party. If I do say so myself, I made a pretty cunning little ugly witch.

The Browning House

This is the house in which I spent most of my elementary and high school years. Once my mother, a widow, became Avalon's postmaster, she was able to get a loan to move from our tiny rental house to what was probably one of the first houses in town to have indoor plumbing. Built by the local banker, S.A. Browning, in 1918, it changed hands a time or two before it became ours about the time I entered the third grade, and was home to my mother while she lived, and then to my eldest brother Donald until he passed away in 2003.

Pictured here as it was originally built, complete with the concrete hitching post in front at the street, it was later covered with white vinyl siding. Upstairs consisted of three bedrooms and a bath, occupied by Mom, myself, and whichever brother was living at home at the time. My brothers, Jerry and Donald, ten and fourteen years older respectively, were at various times gone, either in the military (Air Force and Marines) or in college, or married (for a while). So it was usually Mom and me getting on each others nerves, as mother and daughter will do.

My mother had the proverbial green thumb, and there were house plants and flower beds and a good-sized vegetable garden which gave me my love of plants and growing things. And most of all, there were books. It must be in the DNA, since I was always told stories about my dad who, when sent out to plow with the team of horses, could be found parked at the end of a row, reading. Both my brothers were reading almost any time they weren't tormenting me; my mother read, and read to me until I was old enough to read myself; and then I was an avid patron of the Chillicothe Library, and in Avalon, of the regular stops of their bookmobile.

Our water was supplied by a cistern outside at the back of the house. Rain water was collected through eaves and downspouts into the well. My mother was insistent at one point (my brothers rolling their eyes) she had to have a look into the well to see what was down there. A thick concrete slab covered the opening, and could be removed only by some determined pushing and swearing. Mom was horrified to learn that there was a snake of some sort (along with maybe a frog? dead mouse?) in the water, and quickly had my brothers replace the top. She supposed it hadn't had any adverse affects on us to that point, so as disturbing as it must have been to her, we never heard any more about it. I credit my still healthy immune system and gut flora to the stimulus of the cistern water I imbibed until I went away to college.

One day recently I was doing some of what my Grandma Jesse used to refer to as 'ridding and sorting' and came across the abstract for the lots on which both our house and the school grounds were built. My brother Donald later purchased two lots of the old school property. It seems the Browning house may have been on the block which once held the graves of the family of Wesley Scott, for whom the town's location—Scott's Mound—was originally named. The Browning house remains, although much remodeled both inside and out by families who have resided there since. Although I have an abundance of fond memories and hardly any bad ones of the house, I have no desire to revisit it.

You can't really ever go home again.

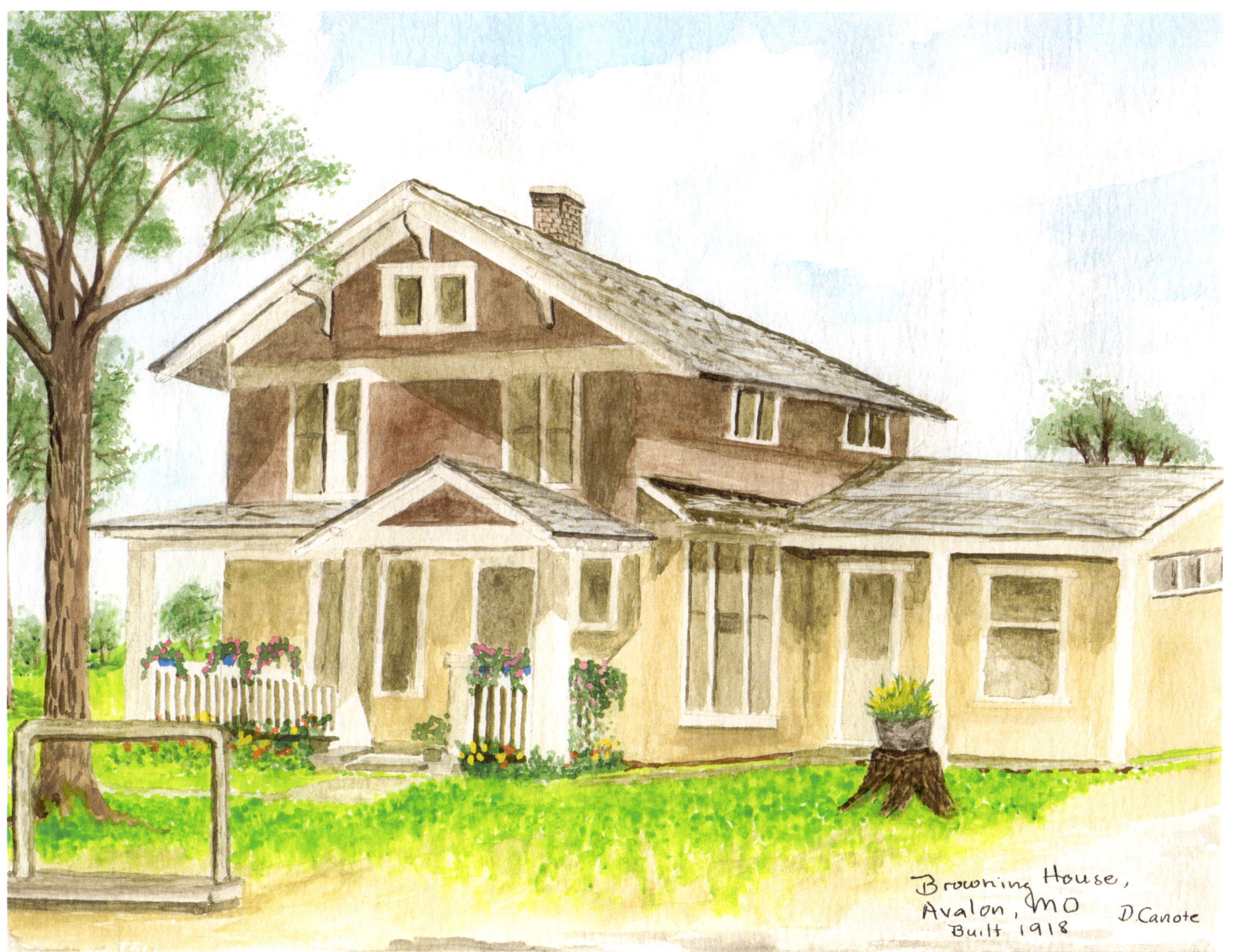
Browning House,
Avalon, MO
Built 1918
D.Canote

Avalon College

My maternal grandparents, Van Dorn Fullerton and Jesse (Dunlap) Fullerton, were both of Scottish descent, with a bit of English and Irish added in. That may be why I was reared as a Presbyterian. As with most small, rural communities, much of Avalon's social life revolved around its two churches, the Methodist, which was next door to our house, and the Presbyterian, my spiritual home.

The large old brick structure where we went to church every Sunday was originally built in 1869 as the Avalon Academy, which advanced to a college in 1881. The institution of our church itself was also founded in 1869, but Presbyterian services were first conducted in what was then Fairview School, a tiny one-room building two miles north and one mile west of Avalon. In 1875, a new church building was built in Avalon, and was subsequently sold in 1891 to the congregation of the First Methodist Church, at which time the Presbyterians bought the Avalon College building. The Presbyterian Church was eventually dissolved in Avalon as its membership diminished along with the town's population. This old and venerable building was sold to a local resident who removed the second story and remodeled it into a home.

Located on the northernmost lots of the town, the large brick structure sat on the highest point of the town, which was also the elevated location formerly known as Scott's Mound. Old photos taken at different times show a two-story and later, an imposing three-story building, topped at the front by an open bell-tower. The third and top story, added some years after the initial construction, caught fire and burned, leaving the building again with two stories and the repaired bell tower.

As I recall, there were two wood frame outhouses—*Men* and *Women*—located on the north side, out of sight, of course. At the time we attended church, the surrounding ground was covered by lush bluegrass with several large walnut trees providing shade for the annual church picnics and vacation bible school.

With a limited population of cohorts living in Avalon during my childhood, I spent a lot of time alone, exploring and discovering—streams with little fish and tadpoles, springs bubbling out of the shallow sandy road ditches—north of town. At some point I noticed in back of the church what appeared to be a linear depression, lined on both sides by well-grown trees and overgrown along its length with less mature trees and brush. It ran east to west across town, remnants of an old roadway, abandoned when there was no longer enough use to justify its upkeep.

Recently I saw photographs of one of the old trails, eroded deeply across the west by the trail of wagon trains that carried settlers to the Great Plains and beyond, and I thought about that old roadway from my childhood. Livingston County history records the passage of the Mormons across Scott's Mound, so it is possible their wagon wheels also passed where I had walked. I wondered about the lives that passed along the roadway during its existence, and the passing of those lives along with memories of that time. It made me aware of the passing of my own life, and what memories I hold that will likewise pass with my death.

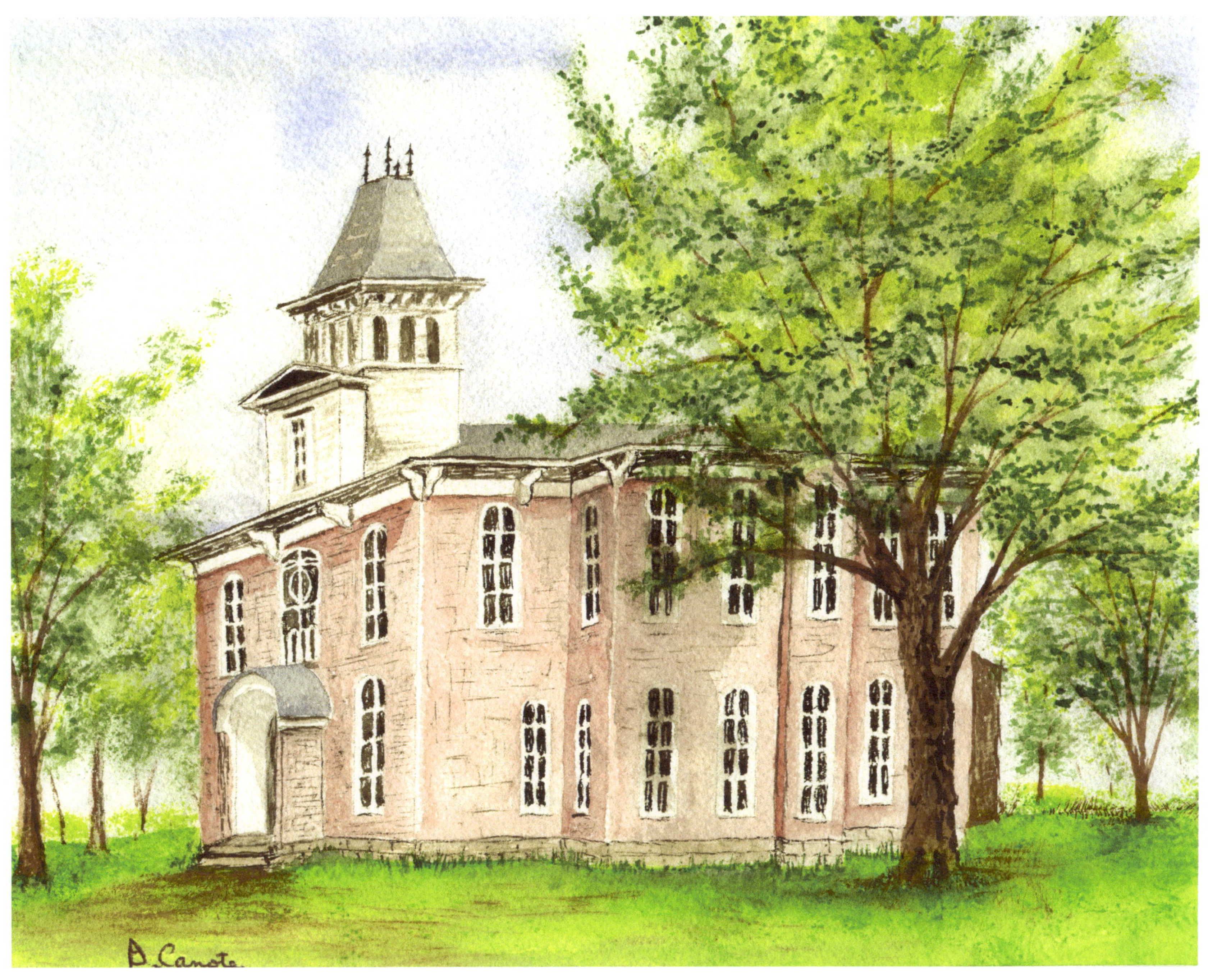
B. Canote

The Avalon Mill

The photo I used for this building came from another old Avalonian I have the joy of seeing on the increasingly rare occasions of a death in our closely related family. If you can bear some of my family history, Gary Rickenbrode is a first cousin of my first cousin, Louise (Canning) Barlow, whose mother was my mother's sister. Gary's mother, Helen (Canning) Rickenbrode, was Louise's aunt, sister to Louise's father, Carmel Canning. I mention this relationship specifically because these individuals, Gary and Louise, both with steel trap minds, were always my go-to source of information for all things related to family and Avalon history. Louise has now passed, but Gary remains a veritable gusher of information.

While the old building in the photo was not particularly interesting or attractive, it was absolute proof of the existence of such a structure. When my Grandmother Jesse passed, we found among her things a poem entitled "Avalon Had A Watermill," which we presume she had written. Now this was a bit curious, since the town sits on a prominent elevation with respect to the surrounding land and, while the area surrounding the town has small springs that bubble up in sandy road ditches, nowhere is there a stream of sufficient volume to drive a waterwheel. At one of our yearly Avalon Reunions I asked Gary if he was aware of there ever being such a mill. He mused a moment, and then responded that indeed he thought there was, although probably it was driven by steam rather that water.

This project has driven me to dip further and further into the history of my home town, as well as Missouri history in general. Searching for references to Avalon's mill, I learned a bit more about mills in general, so being a teacher by avocation, I feel obliged, in turn, to educate my reader.

A mill is in general a device that operates to mechanically transform some mineral or raw agricultural material into a more refined product. While small milling devices were traditionally used on farms and homesteads, they were also expanded into commercial enterprises made profitable by an economy of scale and by the fact that it was more convenient for the consumer to pay for such a service than to do it himself.

Saw mills cut trees into boards, producing rough-sawn lumber. Older construction used this lumber extensively, especially in rural areas, and it is still used to build barns, sheds, fences, and the mill shown in the painting. Saw mills, especially in Amish country, are profitable businesses in many locales, since lumber is a commodity still much in demand.

Carding mills have typically been located in areas where fiber animals such as sheep and goats are raised. These mills process the wool into fibers that can then be woven into cloth. I didn't research these mills in detail, but have had the opportunity to visit the Watkins Woolen Mill near Kearney, Missouri. Dating from 1860, the mill is a historic site and still operates. It is beautifully maintained and worth the time to visit.

The Avalon mill was a grist mill, operating a pair of grinding wheels to turn wheat into flour or corn into cornmeal. *The History of Livingston County*, 1886, records the construction of a steam-powered flouring mill on the west of Avalon in 1879. Its presence is also confirmed in *The Encyclopedia of the History of Missouri, Volume I*, by H.L. Conard, 1901. Conard says of Avalon, "It had a large flouring mill, a newspaper, and about ten shops in different trades." The population of Avalon was given as approximately five hundred, so it would have definitely been a viable enterprise for the community.

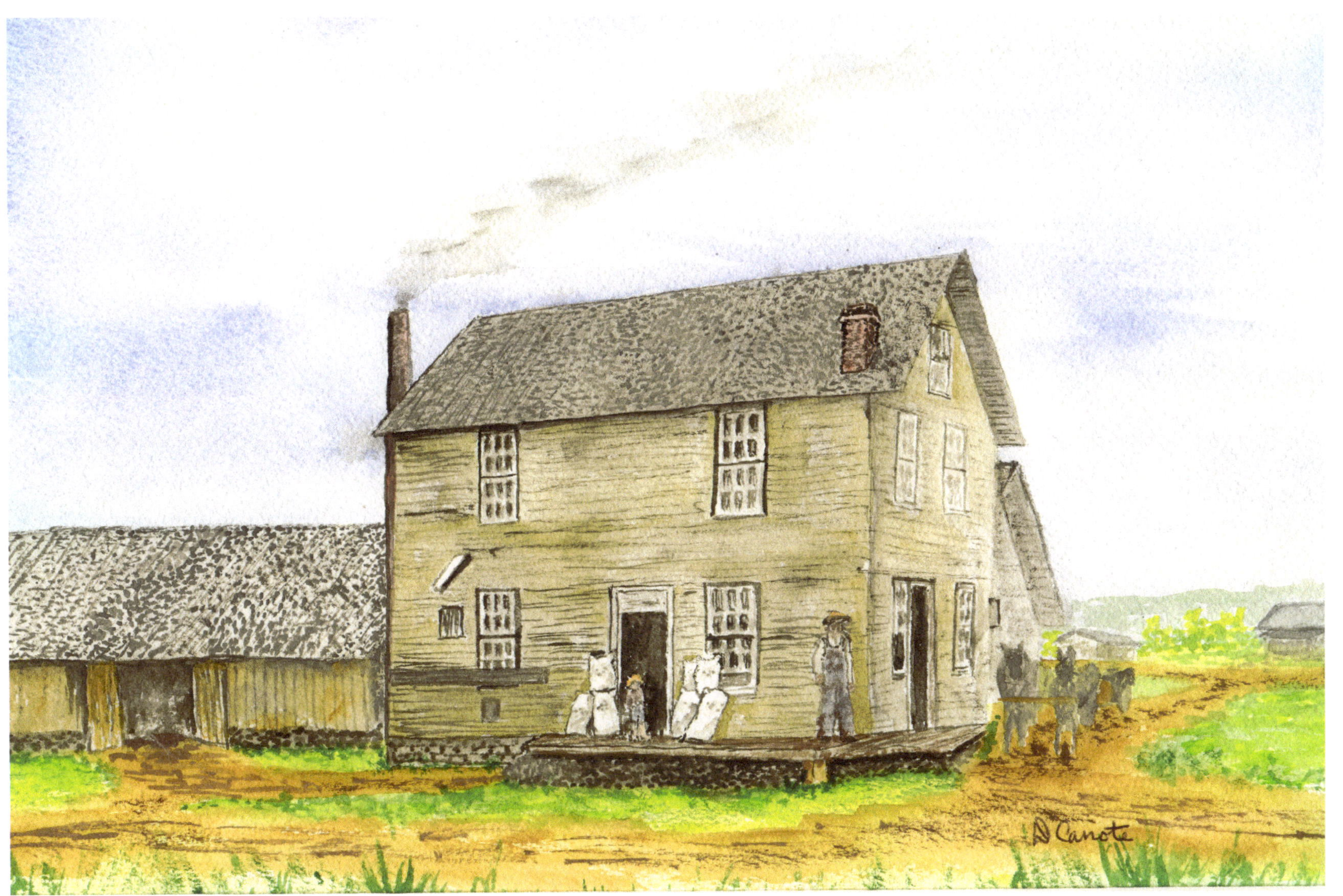
D Canote

In forested areas, wood would have been the most common fuel; however, again according to Gary, Avalon also had a nearby coal mine, and he even knew the location! What?! Another eye-opening discovery about my little town. I checked out the history of coal mining in Missouri and found that there have been and still are shallow deposits of bituminous coal scattered throughout many of the northern counties. While they served local needs for a time, it has since become unprofitable to mine and sell from these sources.

Having hopefully enlightened my reader, I will close with a copy of my grandmother's poem. I like to think that, had she had the time in her busy life—raising a family, sewing for and feeding five children and a husband, keeping a garden, chickens, a milk cow, and all the other challenges of life in a rural community in the late 1800s and early 1900s—she might also have written some interesting stories. She certainly wrote enough postcards and letters to friends and family to have filled quite a lot of books.

Avalon Had a Watermill
Jesse Fullerton
1969

O listen to the water mill,
through all the livelong day,
As the turning of the wheel
wears hour by hour away.
How languidly the autumn wind
does stir the weathered leaves,
As on the field the reaper sings,
while binding up the sheaves.
A solemn proverb strikes my mind
and as a spell is cast,
The wheel will never turn again
with water that has passed.

The Avalon Odd Fellows Lodge

Of all the buildings that were a part of my childhood in Avalon, this one has a strong significance for me. Before I tell you about that, let me say something about the building and its place in our community.

Like nearly all such fraternal organizations, the Independent Order of the Odd Fellows (IOOF) has been around for a long time. Originating in England in the 1700s, its U.S. equivalent was founded in 1819 in Baltimore. With its mandate to "... visit the sick, relieve the distressed, bury the dead, and educate the orphan," its members filled an important benevolent niche in our small town. They were the first such fraternal order to include females, the Rebekahs, to which my mother belonged.

Certain fundraisers were held throughout the year, most notable among them being periodic 'coon hunts. Hosted by the IOOF, whose lodge sat on Main Street on the corner of the block just east of my home, we had a front row seat, so to speak, for the comings and goings over the weekend event. Men and boys (and a few women) from miles around would bring their 'coon dogs and descend on nearby woods, fields, and the like in an attempt to tree the wily raccoon. That process is worth a whole book chapter in itself, but not here. As much as these hunts were joyfully anticipated by the area good ol' boys, there were dreaded by the town residents, who could look forward to little sleep while the baying of hounds and the noise of pickup trucks continued throughout the night.

That's all I have to say about the Odd Fellows. So then, you wonder, what makes the building special enough to paint? Well, there happened to be a boy in town that was part of my life then and remained a friend throughout our entire lives, until his death a few years ago.

Probably somewhere in my second year of school, soon after moving into the Browning house, I discovered J.R. I suppose I should say we discovered each other since he and I only lived a block apart. We naturally found plenty of things to do together. The streets in town were variously dirt or gravel, so when it rained and the ditches filled with water they made excellent waterways for amateur boat builders, dam makers, frog catchers, and water waders. That was also a time of toy guns, and cowboys and indians (not to be culturally insensitive, it was just the game).

When one of us could escape our respective houses, we would meet on the corner at the lodge building, in front of which there was a cabinet-enclosed set of balance-beam scales, connected below ground to a device for weighing large loads. When a farmer wanted to weigh a load of grain, someone would come and unlock the cabinet, the driver would pull onto the platform, the weight and other information was recorded, the transaction paid for, and the cabinet relocked.

From the time J.R. and I were big enough to climb onto the top of the scales cabinet, that perch became our special property, from which we monitored traffic and other activities on main street and through town, and opined on the limited range of topics we knew enough to talk about.

J.R.'s dad was career Air Force, so periodically he and his family would be gone for several years, then move back for a time, and then leave again. Each time they returned we would renew our friendship, which naturally evolved to a bit of teenage romance in high school before he left again and his family settled in Arizona. From high school, he joined the armed forces, became an Airborne Ranger and served during the Vietnam war, and finally ended up back in Arizona where he worked for the Bureau of Reclamation until he retired.

We kept in touch through his Avalon relatives and infrequent letters, and later in our lives, we met up again, after I had divorced, finished grad school, and had bought a little section of woods with a cabin in Howard County. He flew up for a visit and we spent a few days camping and hiking in the Ozarks and renewing our friendship, both perhaps hoping something might come of it. But we were too far apart in too many ways to become more than friends, and we both recognized that and were okay with it. So he went back to Arizona and we both went on with our lives.

In a way he betrayed me, though. We still kept in touch by email, until I noticed that I hadn't heard anything from him for too long. I searched online and eventually found his obituary. I missed him so much then, and I was so angry! He didn't tell me goodbye.

So if you look at the painting you may see, atop the Fairbanks Scales cabinet, the ghostly glow of two souls perched side by side, perhaps still considering their lives.

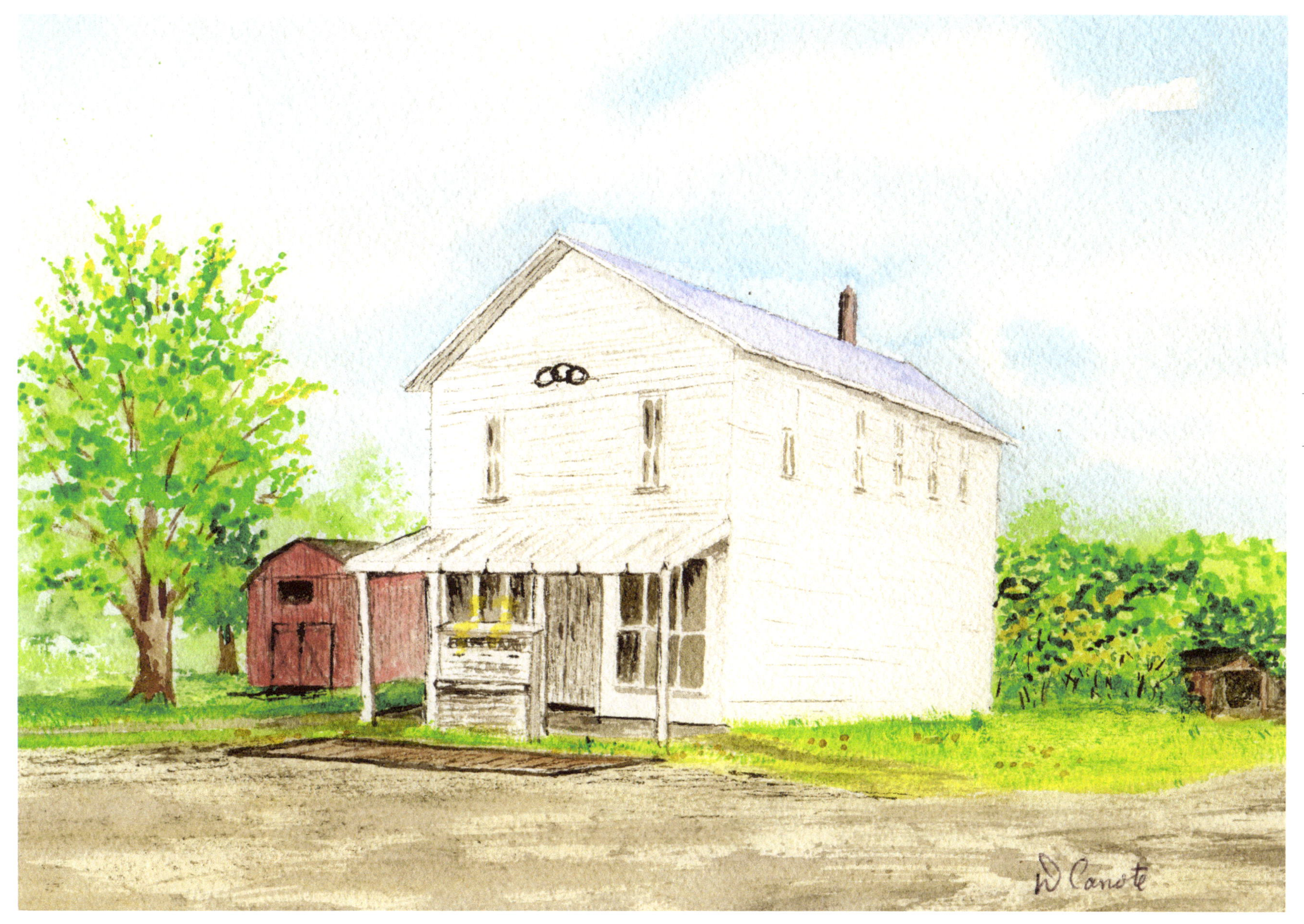
D Canote

Chapter 2

Scenes and Other Sundry Subjects

It's hard to know exactly how to describe the compulsion to create. I have read that sculptors feel there is an image trapped in stone or clay, struggling to break free. Having recently watched Ken Burns's documentary on country music, I think many singers and songwriters feel the same compulsion, another way to express some insistent emotion. Some of the things I paint are like that, something somewhere in my consciousness looking for a way out.

On top of the need to create, there are some subjects, within and beyond the boundaries of my home town, that have pushed at me to be painted. I like to find old black and white photos and paint them in color, sometimes adding summer foliage to winter scenes. Old buildings are especially appealing to me, as well as scenery that displays the forces and variety of nature. And I am constantly looking around me for opportunities to take my own photos of potential subjects.

During the process of photographing subjects to paint, I discovered that painting altered the way I view my subjects. I began to consider perspective, position, background, lighting, and a host of other considerations that influence how I would render the subject as watercolor. I began to understand why so many pictures I saved from vacation trips and special events turned out so uninteresting. How do you capture the majesty of the sweeping vista of a mountain range or desert in a four by six inch photo? The composition of a photo or painting must speak to the observer in a way that compels more than a single glance.

In the narrative that accompanies each paintings in this chapter, I have tried to convey something of the meaning or interest inspired by the subject. And, once a teacher etcetera, I just had to include a tutorial or two.

20

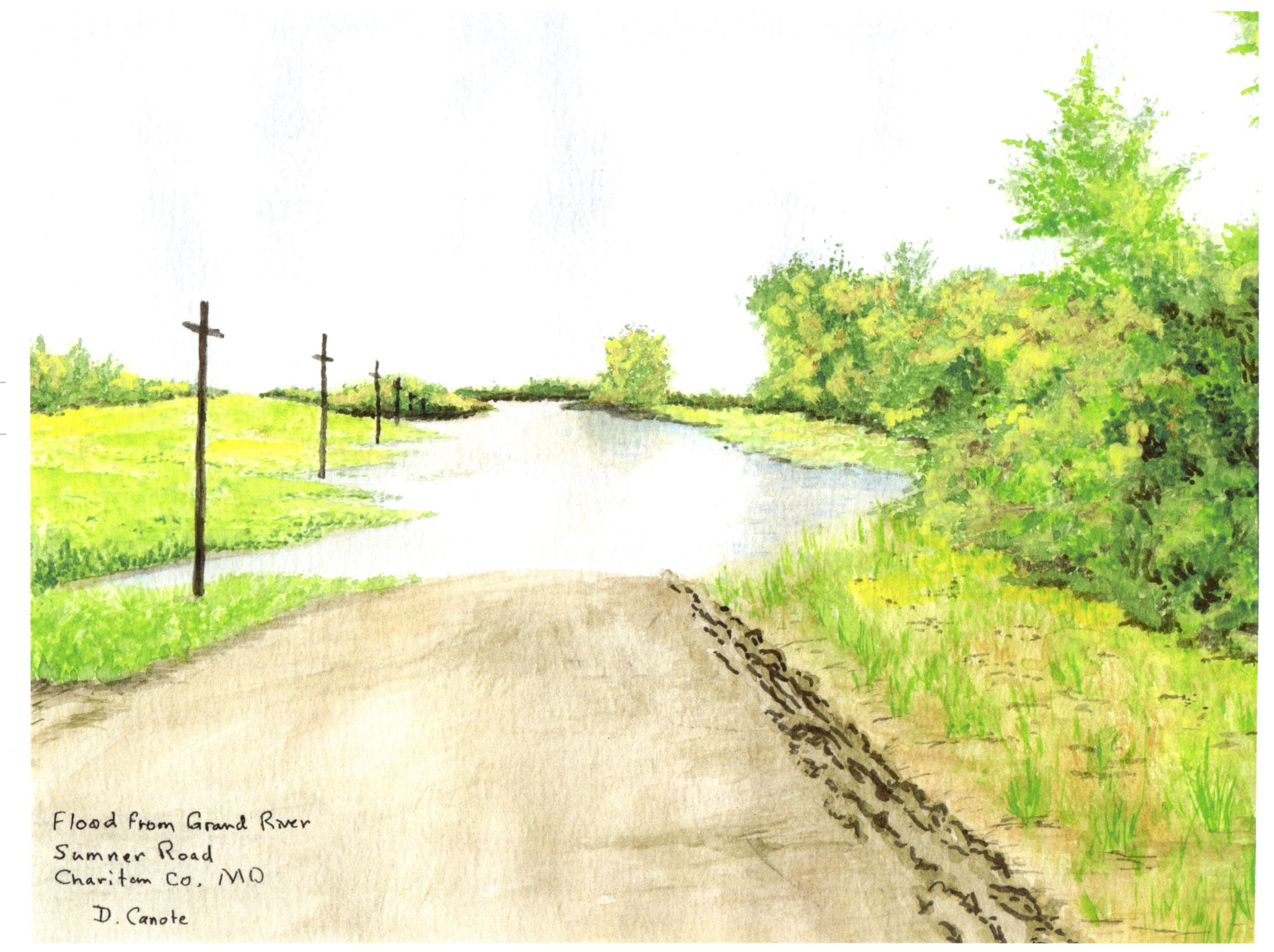

Flooding from the Grand River

Flooding is much on the minds of residents these days, not only in Missouri, but in surrounding areas as well as throughout the world. Global climate effects include greater than usual swings in temperature, more extreme weather events, and a northward creep in average first frost date, leading to changes in agricultural zones. Even for Missouri, where we are accustomed to the unpredictability of weather, it is inevitable that we will see greater impacts on our lifestyles, economy, and freedom of travel.

Where I grew up, in the glaciated northern prairie region of Missouri, flooding was a minor event compared to the experience of those who live and have lived along the Missouri and the Mississippi. Before the wide-scale construction of dams and levees, the annual inundation of riparian fields and communities was the norm, and was an excuse for folks to exercise what author Stephen King has referred to as the "Let's go look at the accident . . . " syndrome. It was a common excuse in the mid twentieth century (or even earlier, I assume) for everyone to load up in a vehicle and go see what the floods were doing. My painting of a 1955 flood near Sumner was done from a photo taken during one of our family outings to check out the flood waters.

If you look at a map of the river systems and watersheds of Missouri, all the rivers and streams in northwestern and central portions of the state flow south into the Missouri. This is, of course, a function or the gradient of the land and the influence of the glacial scouring from the last Ice Age. Of the twenty or so of this region's major streams and rivers, nearly half of them feed into the Grand River, which enters the Missouri at the 'Big Bend' on the northern border of Saline County. The channeling of the waters of these rivers into the Grand, especially in times of large spring and summer rainfall events, produces the effect of trying to evacuate a theater or other large building through a single door following a fire alarm; except that the banks of a river are only a 'suggestion' for the river's channel, and all the excess water takes any path of least resistance into its floodplains, irrespective of whatever humans have put there.

These days, Mother Nature is once again demonstrating to us that our puny efforts to engineer our environment is the perpetual exercise in futility. Every time she flushes the big upstream toilet, we are all going to have plenty of opportunities to gawk, but they will undoubtedly be less and less entertaining and more and more horrific.

Map Source: Missouri Department of Natural Resources

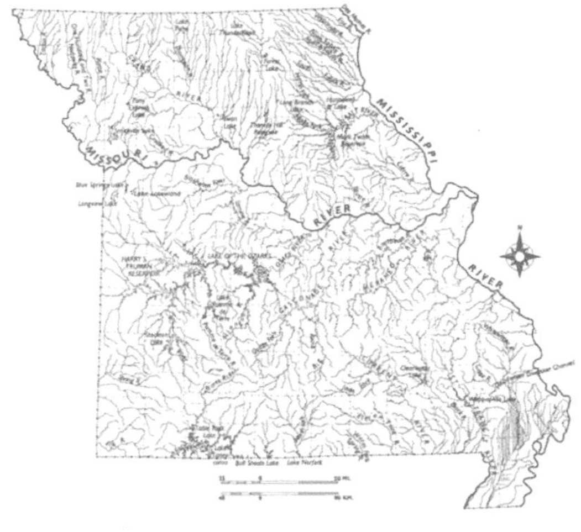

HYDROGRAPHY

Major Water Resources in Missouri

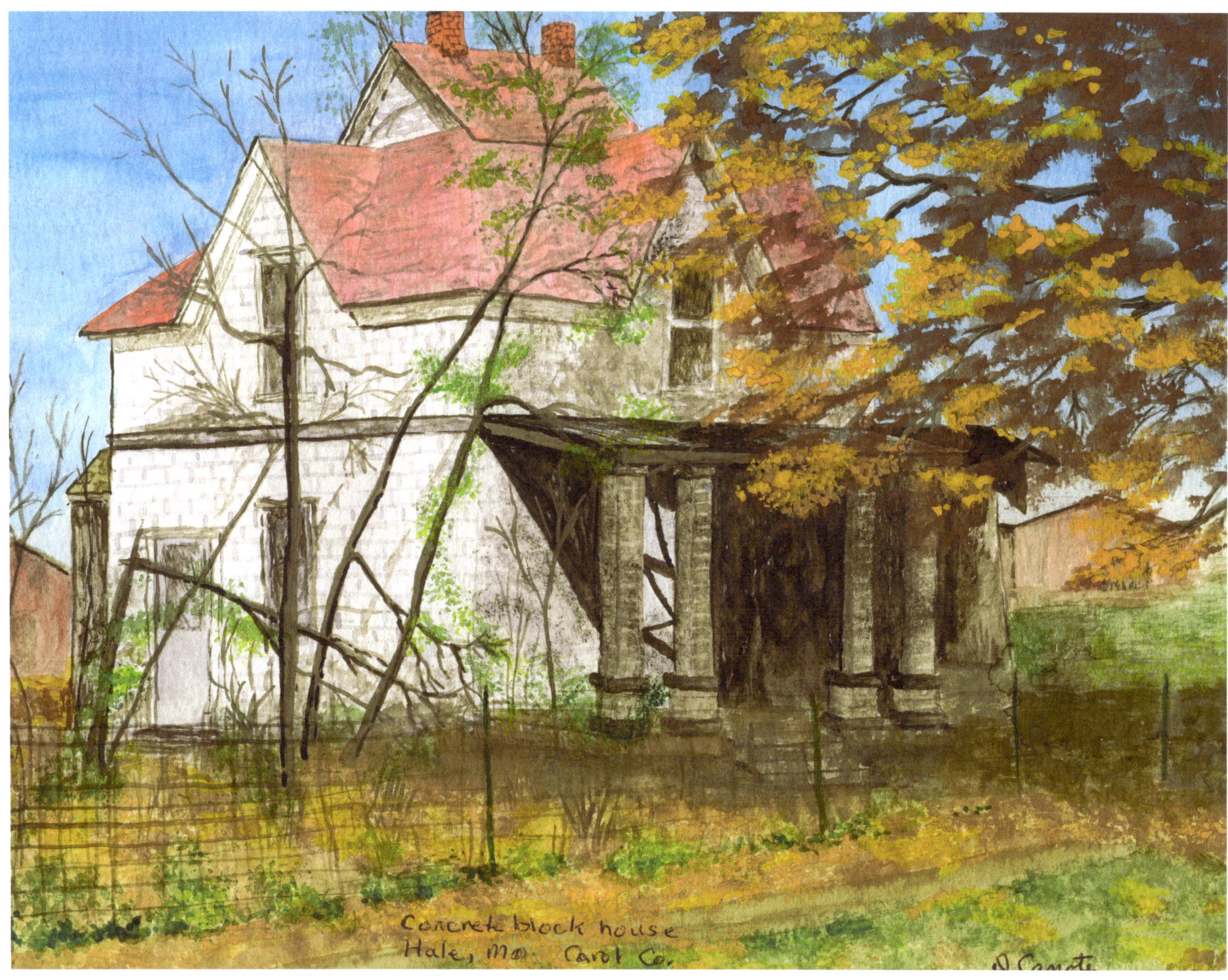
Concrete block house
Hale, Mo. Carol Co.

Old House in Hale, Missouri

Hale is another little town in the northern prairies of Missouri, about ten miles from Avalon. Much larger than Avalon, it still has a K—12 school, a couple of churches, post office, a restaurant and pool hall, grocery, and several other businesses catering to area farmers. I probably missed something, but then I don't now and never did spend much time there. I do know that my father's family lived near Hale, and his picture hangs with those of his graduating classmates in the hall of the school.

My cousin, Mary Louise Barlow, and her husband Tom lived in Hale for some years, and of all my female cousins, she and I probably were closest. She had a wonderful mind and never forgot a thing. We used to visit and I delighted in her recollections of all our family history, to say nothing of everyone else's family history!

It was the custom in our later years to take turns hosting Thanksgiving dinner among her branch of the family. One year, when it was her turn, she had moved from a larger house into a nice but very small housing unit, so she enlisted the lady who owned the local restaurant into cooking us turkey dinner with all the trimmings. The rest of us brought a dessert to share. After the meal, we set out to walk off all the food we had eaten (groan!) by touring the town.

On one street we passed this old house, which for some reason drew my interest enough to take its picture. There was just something about it that made me stand and look, and look, and . . . well, it was kind of haunting—me. So when I got home I had to paint it.

The house was constructed of concrete blocks. They weren't the so-called cinder blocks used today. Rather, they were faceted on the surface to look like they had been hewn from stone. I tried to trace the beginnings of the house but never found out who owned it, so I don't have any stories to pass on. I did find, however, that do-it-yourself block construction was common from the 1890s to 1930s, with blocks made using a Wizard concrete block machine that could be purchased through the Sears and Roebuck catalog for $42.50. Well! Sears really did have everything. You could even order a house from Sears, did you know that? How the mighty have fallen.

Grandma Jesse and Jerry Feeding the Chickens

This painting was done from a black and white photograph, likely taken by my mother, Mary Francis (Fullerton) Deardorff with her little Brownie camera. The camera was never far from her hands and she documented some wonderful scenes from the lives of our family and our community.

Grandma Fullerton was raised in a very proper 'English' manner. I never saw her in other than a neat, well-fitted cotton dress, covered by an apron for everyday chores, and in sturdy walking shoes. When company came, the apron was whipped off, hair was tamed with a wet comb, and hospitality was cordial and polite. This photo may have been taken on a day when she had just returned from church, or a visit to a neighbor, as she had on a small hat of some sort. I never saw her posture other than ramrod straight and I sometimes wondered if she spent her childhood with a book on her head, as we read about in our stories.

As for my brother Jerry, his little tow-headed, barefoot self was the trial of my grandmother's days. He was also somewhat a trial to our oldest brother, Donald, our mother, and his teachers and principal, and in fact, the entire town during his high school days. And that is besides the pain in the rear he was to his little sister for most of his life. But that would be a bunch more stories.

This picture brings to my mind the issues he had with my grandmother's chickens. She tried her best to teach him the chores that had to be done around the house and garden. His job of gathering eggs often resulted in fewer eggs, since he carried them with the tips of his fingers, from which they often ended up—oops!—on the ground. Also, he was simply terrorized by trying to pull an egg out from under a broody hen, which was prone to peck. I wasn't much crazy about that job either.

We did have a huge laugh from a tale over the dinner table at a family get-together when we were all older. Grandma was not present at that time, for whatever reason, and it was probably a good thing. At one time she had a huge red rooster that pretty much had the run of the farm, husbanding the hens and keeping his people on their toes. Since there was no indoor bathroom, when nature called it was necessary to visit the outhouse, which was attached to the end of the chicken house and was reached by a sidewalk through the chicken yard. The rooster would watch for Jerry to come through the gate to reach the outhouse. If he could reach the boy before the boy reached the outhouse, he would jump up and try to spur him or flog him with his huge wings. Jerry hated that rooster, and he carefully plotted his revenge.

Between the house to the south and the outhouse to the north was a smokehouse, used at that time only for storage, with a board-constructed hinged window on the north side. Below the window was a large rock about ten by fourteen inches or maybe a little larger (no idea what its function was, but I recall the rock vividly). When the day came that Jerry had proven he could lift the rock, he hefted it to sit on the ledge of the window, closed the south door, and made a commotion that lured the rooster to the window. There, it looked up, possibly with murder in its beady eye, whereupon the rock 'fell' onto the rooster and ended its reign of terror. Jerry dragged it to the ditch, a repository for all the other unwanted discards of our lives, and Grandma never knew what happened to the rooster.

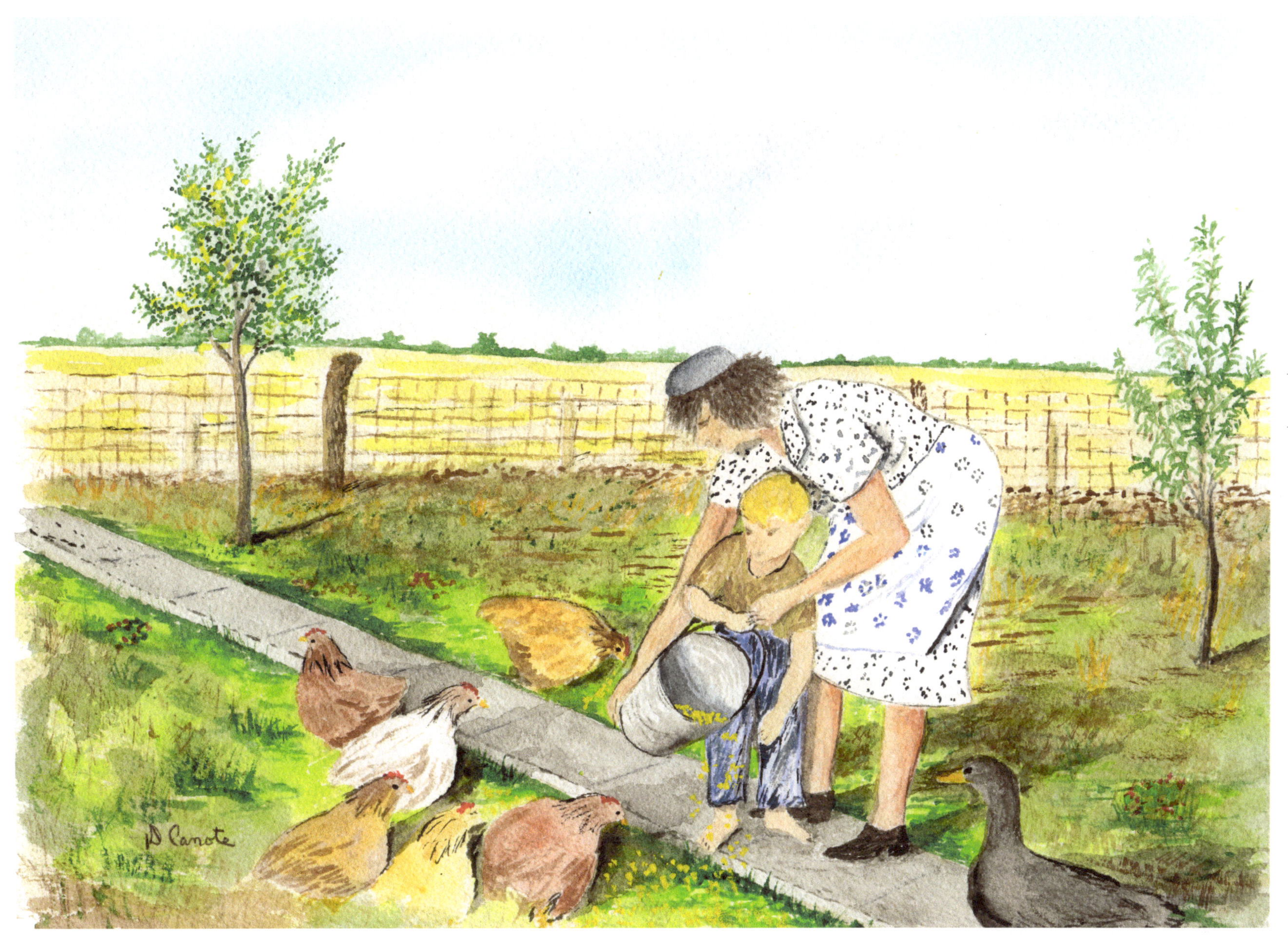
D Canote

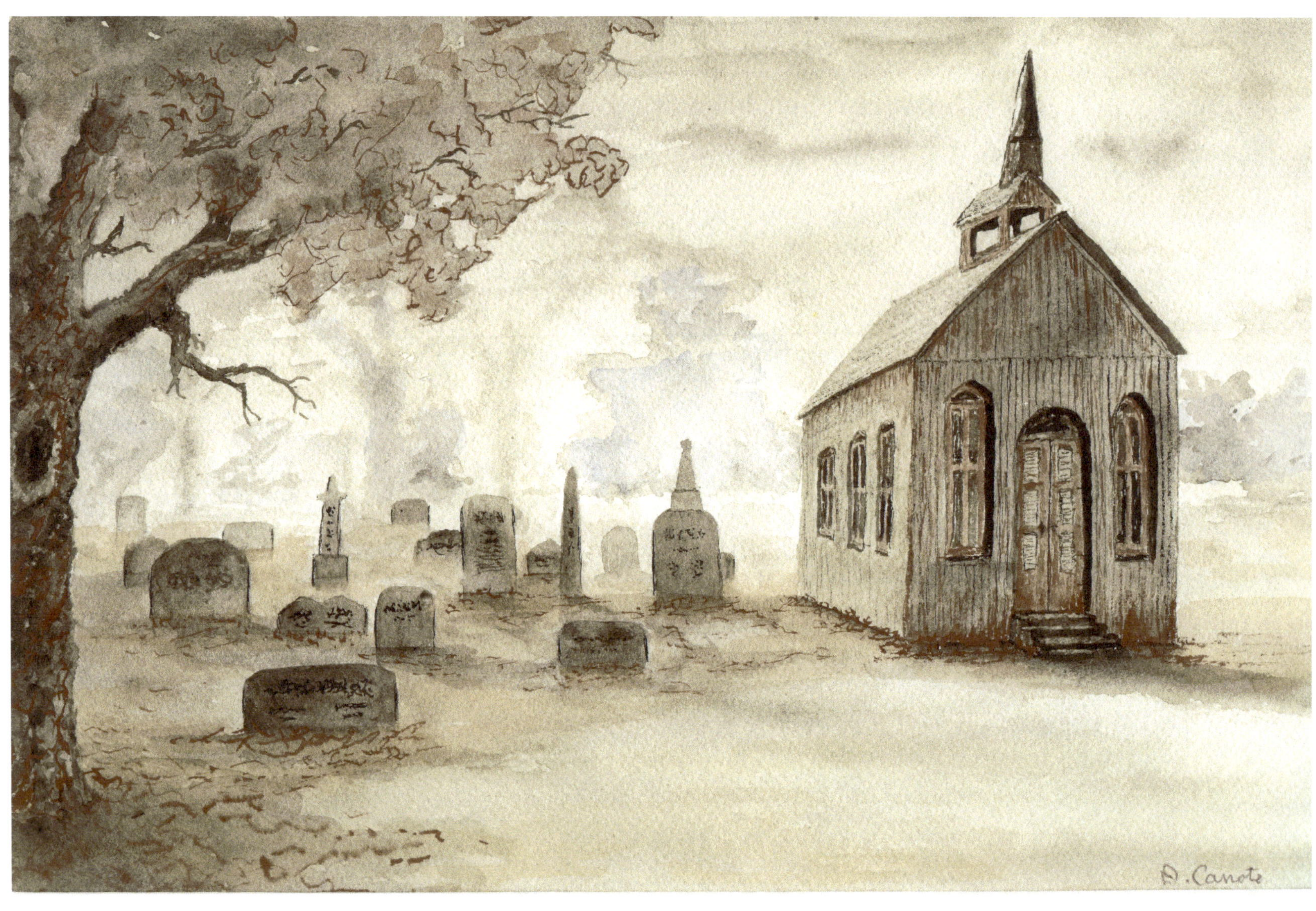
A. Canote

Old Church and Cemetery

Shades of Goth! This scene doesn't exist other than in my imagination. As is often the case when I sit down to paint, I was meandering around in the attic of my memory and it just appeared, like a ghost from an old chest. I suppose I am not alone in my fascination with old churches and cemeteries, as there were a lot of interested comments when I had the painting on display. It seemed to draw more attention than some of what I thought were better paintings, evidence of the more ghoulish side of human nature, perhaps. People love what "creeps them out," as our grandson would say.

It was a common occurrence, when my father's two sisters and their husbands visited from Kansas City, for us all to load up in their big car and visit old rural cemeteries in nearby townships and counties, locating the graves of more distant family members. I recall one isolated graveyard in the midst of a clearing in the woods with very old tombstones, some leaning or broken, and one mausoleum. The concrete lid had been pushed aside, undoubtedly by some mischief-inclined teens, so that you could peer down inside. The bare iron casket was visible, an old style (think Dracula's coffin!) with a glass faceplate such that you could see the bare skull of the deceased. Wooo*eee*oooo!

It was a common practice then, as it is today, to have an open casket for viewing at funerals, and there were quite a lot of deaths throughout my childhood. Death was no mystery to most children in our community—farm animals, pets, and beheading a chicken or two for dinner, as well as farm and highway accidents that maimed and killed a lot of people before there were seat belts and safety devices on implements. Several of the folks on the Avalon Then and Now Facebook page post copies of old newspaper clippings of deaths from bizarre circumstances and even regular events you wouldn't hear about now, such as runaway wagon teams and getting kicked in the head while milking a cow. *Ha!* you think, but if it was you, well . . .

The cemetery is just south of Avalon on what would originally have been a high stretch of wide open prairie. My grandfather, Van Fullerton was a big barrel-chested man, who served as Avalon Cemetery custodian for a time, and my Uncle Jim, my mom's brother, told a story about his dad having been called upon to dig a grave. Needing to have it done the following day, Grandpa was hard at work in the dark with a lantern, down in the grave hole, throwing dirt out over the top, when a person walked past the cemetery on his way home. Grandpa, being a good Scottish Presbyterian, accompanied his work by hymn singing, and his strong bass voice was rolling out of the grave with "When the roll is called up yonder . . . ," resulting in the traveler making it home in record time.

I named this painting *Faith of Our Fathers*, accompanying us as it often does from baptism to death. The graves of my parents, maternal grandparents, one brother, aunts, uncles, cousins, and a host of friends and neighbors from my childhood are all there in the Avalon Cemetery, and I try to visit them once a year and remember their lives. We only exist as long as someone holds us in their memories. Perhaps I don't actually remember all those dead folks, but I honor the fact of their lives, and wonder what life was like for them in their time. Live on, old ones, live on!

Vaughn School

A photo of this old school was posted on Facebook by a former schoolmate who lived in the area of the abandoned school building. It spoke to me the way old buildings are wont to do, with the character of its weathered siding, its empty windows and schoolyard, now grown to pasture. Livingston County archives provide a fairly extensive description of its history, a story that will evoke memories in those readers who grew up in rural communities and are old enough to recall the one-room school.

The first school on this site was established in 1870, forty-nine years after Missouri became a state. The school was named after David Vaughn, a former Avalon resident who laid out the district, helped build the school, and served as its first director. The original south-facing building was thirty by forty feet with an anteroom. Average school attendance in the early years was seventy-five to one hundred pupils. The building was also the center for community events and activities, including weekly meetings of the literary society, debates, and musical performances.

The old school was torn down and this painting is of the new school built there in 1910, which still stands several miles west of Avalon. A seventeen-foot-deep cistern provided water which was pulled up in a cedar bucket, and a common dipper was used for drinking. The room was lit by kerosene lanterns when ambient light was insufficient. The Facebook site called Avalon Missouri – Then and Now is dedicated to remembering and connecting the inhabitants of the town and its surrounding communities. Both past and recent posts have revealed that memories and tales of this old school are still extant, evoking a fondness and nostalgia for a shared past.

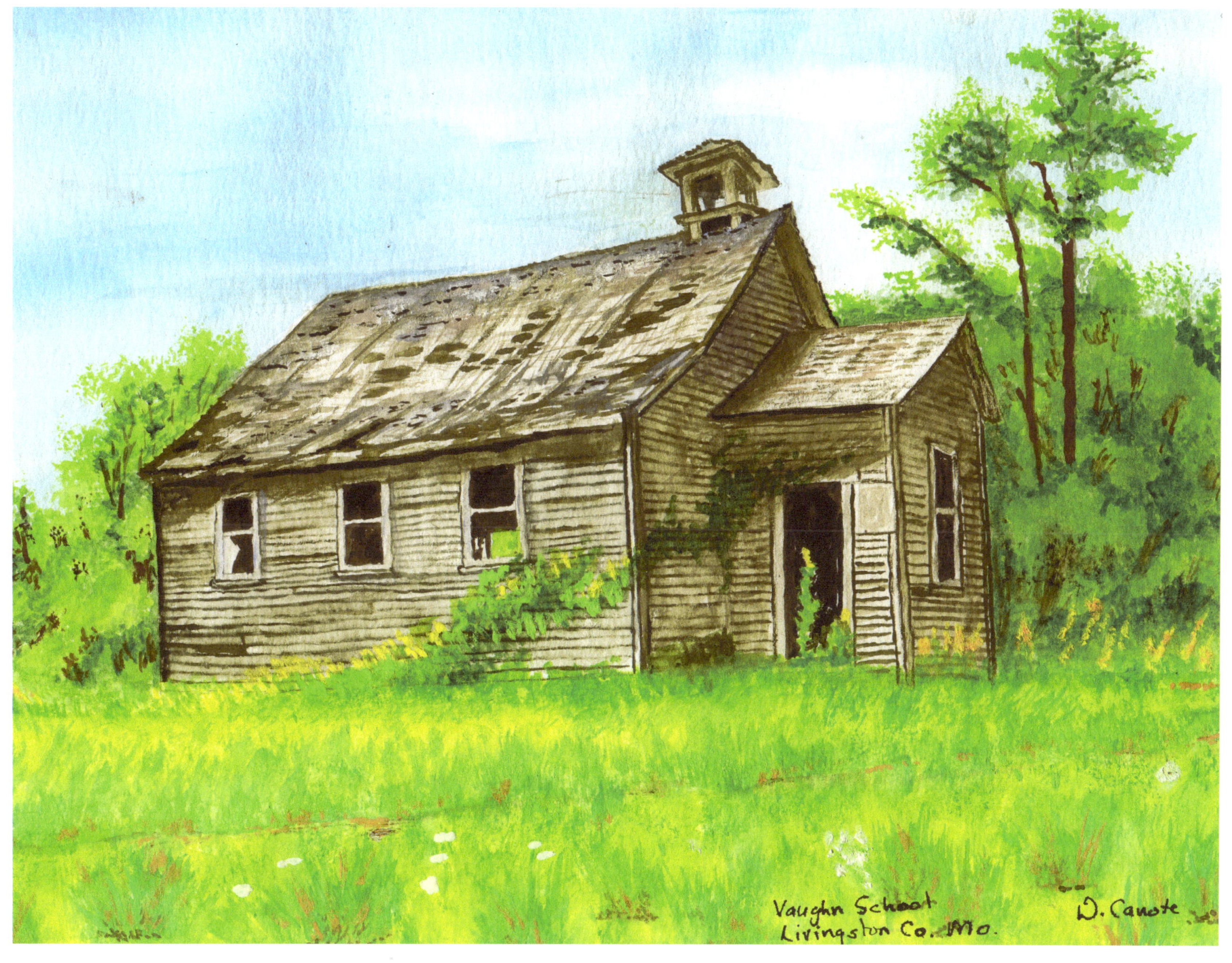
Vaughn School
Livingston Co. Mo.
D. Canote

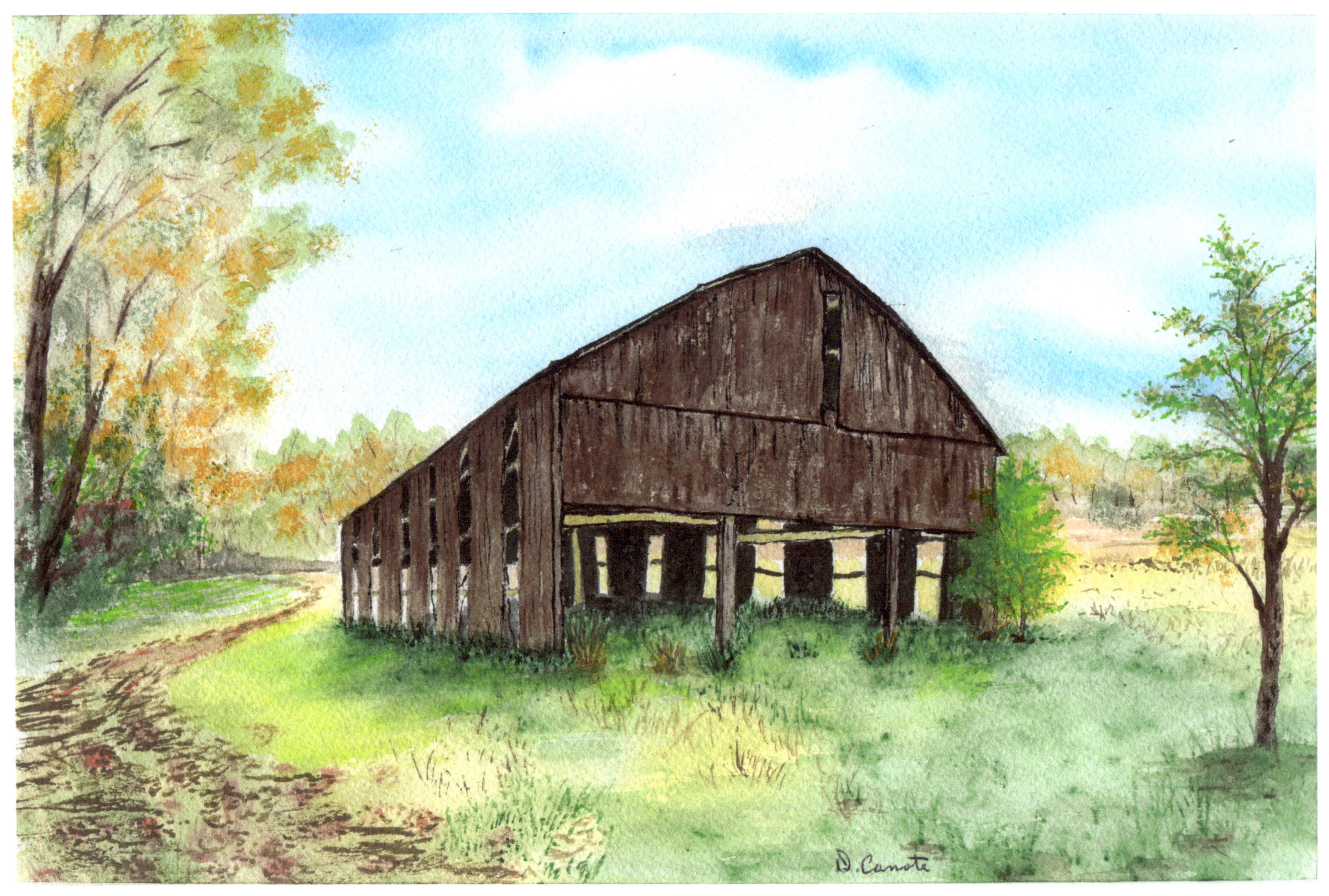
D. Canote

Tobacco Barn

This old barn is located off a gravel road in Chariton County, south of Keytesville, Missouri. The painting was done from a photograph taken by Stephen Bybee, a very talented local Columbia photographer and friend.

The history of tobacco and its use stems from its discovery by European explorers to the New World. The genus *Nicotiana* includes at least nine native tobacco species in the Americas, and excavations at archaeological sites provide evidence of the use of native tobaccos perhaps as early as 6000 B.C.E. It didn't take long for its use to spread back to Europe, and the leaf became a part of the trans-Atlantic trade.

Tobacco itself is an interesting plant. A member of the same family as tomatoes, peppers, and eggplants, it is susceptible to and a host for all the kinds of insect and disease pests that plague those crops. The leaves, however, produce significant levels of nicotine, the alkaloid stimulant that gives the genus its name.

It happened one year while I was still teaching biology at Hickman High School that I had an opportunity to grow some tobacco plants in my home garden. There is a recessive mutation for albinism in the leaf that is useful for demonstrating gene inheritance, so Kathleen Metter, another of our biologists, had her students sprout the seeds in petri dishes in the lab. Of course, since albino plants don't produce chlorophyll, about twenty five percent of the seeds died after germination. Kathleen was ready to discard the remaining fifty five sprouts, having demonstrated the point of a lethal mutation, so I begged the survivors from her, took them home, and planted them in little pots of soil. Every single one of them rooted and produced healthy plants! I transplanted them out side and watched them grow and bloom for the rest of the summer.

Normally, commercial tobacco production involves removing the terminal flower bud to destroy apical dominance and stimulate the bushiness of leaf production. Suckers are removed, just as we often do with tomatoes, to encourage the growth and enlargement of the remaining leaves. This work is all done by hand, and workers in the tobacco fields encounter significant exposure to nicotine from the resinous leaves, necessitating the use of gloves and long pants and sleeves for protection.

Since I had no desire to go through the laborious process of actually producing smokable tobacco, or to prolonged contact with the sticky leaves, I left the plants to flower and enjoyed the arrival of all the hummingbirds and sphinx moths, the main pollinators drawn to the large and attractive tubular pink blooms.

From what I can gather reading about historical production of tobacco, the leaves were originally dried in traditional windowless smoke houses. Most early rural farmsteads included a smoke house to preserve domestic meats and game. A variety of woods produced smoke to give distinctive flavors to the meats hung from rafters in these heated, closed buildings as they dried and cured. We still favor our apple-, hickory-, and mesquite-smoke flavored bacon, hams, BBQ and other meats. At some point it was discovered that air drying produced a superior smoking tobacco, so tobacco barn design progressed from the small, closed, heated structure to a large, well-ventilated barn characterized by those we still see on drives down rural Missouri back roads. And to tie up the story, in case you ever heard the term, a mutation discovered on a Kentucky plantation in 1864 resulted in the light-colored *burley* tobacco since grown for use in cigarettes.

Now times have changed again, and as the government has phased out price support and supply quotas, it is no longer profitable for most growers to spend the laborious two hundred to three hundred hours per acre to bring the leaf to market. In addition, we now recognize the adverse health effects of smoking and the monetary costs of treating smoking-related diseases, so the use, and hence the demand for tobacco has dropped significantly.

But the big, empty barns still remain, largely unused but not unloved, as we appreciate their testimony of our country's history.

Saint Catherine of Siena Mission

This painting was done from a photograph I took on a trip to New Mexico. More about the trip will follow, but first a few things about the church itself and its environs.

Established in 1884, there isn't much to the small former mining town of "Old" Hachita, New Mexico. With an original population of about three hundred residents, it is pretty much a ghost town now, having had its population siphoned off to "New" Hachita to the east when railroad tracks were laid down there. The sole claim to fame of Old Hachita is in having been the base of an expedition in 1916 in retaliation to Pancho Villa's raid on Columbus, New Mexico in that year.

The original building, once a high school building, was purchased by a New York businessman who remodeled it and named the resulting Catholic mission after the patron saint of his mother. The church was later abandoned and is closed up, but its striking appearance in such an-out-of-the-way place was worth the time to photograph.

Hachita is located on New Mexico Hwy 9, about forty-four miles west of Columbus. My eldest daughter, Angela, was about half way through a nine-year Ph.D. project studying native pollinators for the desert agave plant. This involved several years of field study, starting with the Big Bend area and finishing up in the New Mexico boot heel. Angela and I, along with a fellow grad student, exchanged her vehicle for a larger, more rugged four-wheel-drive Tahoe in order to haul all the camping gear and paraphernalia needed for research.

Also known as the century plant, *Agave americana* has a life span of ten to thirty years. Just before it dies, the huge plant, a six-to-ten-foot wide rosette, sends out a tall, branched flowering stalk up to thirty feet high. It is necessary to hang enticing baited traps on the branches of these stalks in the evening in order to catch night-flying insects visiting the flowers. Bats are also frequent and significant pollinators and are mutualistic in their relationship with the agave, feeding on the sweet nectar (22 percent sugar) and on the pollen trapped in their fur and consumed during grooming.

We traveled south from Albuquerque and passed through Hachita to connect with Hwy 81 on our way to a study site just a few miles north of the border town of Antelope Wells. The study site was about a quarter mile off Hwy 81 in a flat desert valley between the Little Hatchet Mountains and the Apache Hills. We left the blacktop highway and drove along a rutted track until we reached the study site. We set up camp—tents, tables, etcetera—and proceeded to get the insect traps up, a process involving long poles with hooks, and other contraptions. Finally, after having eaten a bite, we sacked out for the night. Well I did, the two grad students were in and out several times, switching out traps, and other research related tasks.

The next day, we monkeyed with traps, collected data, and started to worry. I didn't mention it before, but it was late August and in New Mexico, that means it's about time for the monsoons to set in. "What?" you say. Yes indeed, and the caliche clay flats between the mountains are not where one wants to be when that happens. As the clouds closed in my sharp-witted daughter made an executive decision and said, "We have thirty minutes to pack up and get out of here." I said, "We'll never get it done in thirty minutes." Which goes to show how much we can underestimate our kids, because we *did* make it out in thirty minutes with no time to spare. The rain started just as we got back on the blacktop.

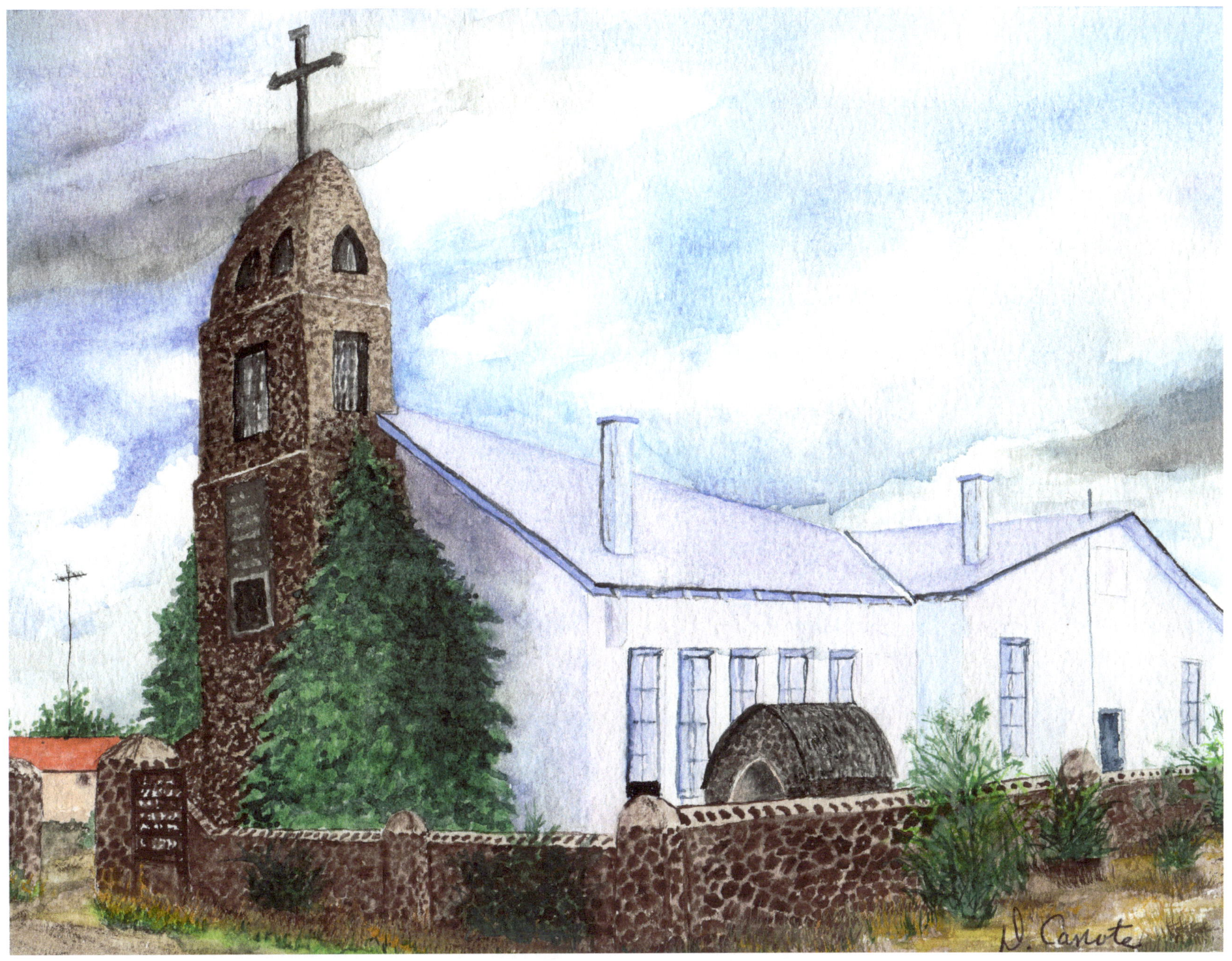

For those who have never been in these kinds of locations, you may not be aware of certain facts: there are no drainage ditches, just road, shoulder, desert; a basin in this kind of country is referred to as a *playa*, which is defined by Merriam Webster as "the flat-floored bottom of an undrained desert basin that becomes at times a shallow lake." Within about twenty minutes the whole flat between the mountains was about axle deep in water, the actual road location a mystery. I was about to lose it when a set of headlights came up behind us, pushing a wave of water in front, passed us and moved right on out. It was the Border Patrol, also having made a wise executive decision, and we followed them until we finally got to a point that was no longer under water.

While at painting group one day, a discussion ensued about our offspring, and the fact that, while we acknowledge they are now adults, we still don't believe they really know how to drive. And I thought about that hair-raising jaunt through the New Mexico desert, and how in awe I was of my daughter steering that big-assed SUV through the flood in apparent calm while her colleague and I sat like deer in the headlights. Wow, I thought proudly, she really has grown up.

Chapter 3
Painting Bridges

The first painting I did of a bridge was the Old Bedford Bridge in Livingston County, now long gone but still fondly recalled by those who lived in the community. Something about the process of painting the bridge made me start a search for more information about the structure of the bridge, which opened the whole figurative can of worms.

In the process of researching bridges I hit the jackpot at the web site called Bridge Hunter. What an amazing resource! The site is a repository for information on historic and notable bridges all across the United States. It is searchable by state, as well as design, status, builder, and other criteria. Photos of bridges from this site are the inspiration for several of the paintings in my book. Credit is given to the photographer or source for each bridge I painted.

The process of learning is often like a seed sprouting or a flower opening, revealing more and more of the true nature inherent in the idea. The concept of a bridge seems pretty simple, but the engineering behind its construction appeals to me as a scientist and a teacher.

Beginning with library resources, I expanded to online sites and even bought several books to add to my already overburdened book shelves. I started with the design of a bridge, then worked my way through the history of their materials and their importance to history itself. I certainly don't intend to write a book about bridges, but it is difficult to explain the paintings without giving a bit of background on each. The individual bridges themselves don't have a particular significance to me, but again, the idea of what each bridge represents does. Thanks to all I learned in the process, I will never look at bridges in the same way again. And I hope you won't either.

The paintings I chose to do all represent, insofar as possible, different construction and design types, and materials. Briefly, Merriam Webster's Dictionary defines a bridge as "a structure carrying a pathway or roadway over a depression or obstacle." The first bridges were built of materials available—logs, stones, and vines—depending on the nature of the depression or obstacle. Materials subject to natural destructive forces such as decay and floods have left no trace of those first bridges, although their evidence remains in the customs of native people whose building techniques have been passed from one generation to the next.

Bridge Terminology

It isn't necessary to know all the terms used for bridges, but it is instructive and fun to be able to look at a bridge and identify some of its common parts. Bridges are broadly encompassed by one of four designs, described below.

- Beam—Solid or *box girders* (hollow beams) are supported by driven vertical columns or *piles*. Intermediate supports for adjacent ends of two bridge spans are *piers*.
- Arch—Self explanatory, the arch transfers a vertical load through its curve to supports at either end called *abutments*.
- Cantilever—The *deck* (surface) of the bridge is supported by piers in its center, much like a seesaw.
- Suspension—The deck is supported from above by ropes, cables or chains hanging from towers.

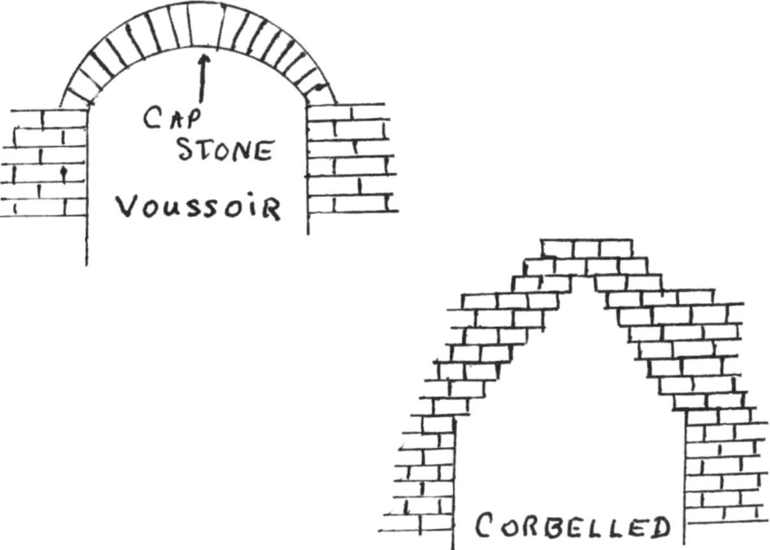

Within and among these broad designs, other terms describing bridge construction are specific to certain designs and materials.

Truss—a framework of members in tension (pulling forces) and compression (pushing forces). Geometrically, the triangle is recognized for its strength, thus members of a truss are assembled in triangular arrangements. The earliest trusses were built of wood, followed later by iron, steel, and in most recent times by carbon polymers. Within this category there is a wide variation in the way these trusses are assembled.

Arch terms

- Where an arch is below and supports the deck, the upper surface of the curve of an arch is called the *extrados*, the inner curve is the *intrados*. The area above the extrados and below deck level is called the *spandrel*, which may be open (see-through) or closed (solid).
- Stone arches act to support the road above. The design forming the arch may be:
    - *corbelled*, with the one end of the stone hanging in space and the other held by the weight of the stones above it,
    - or *voussoir*, with wedge-shaped stones forming the arch itself, finished at the top by a *capstone*.

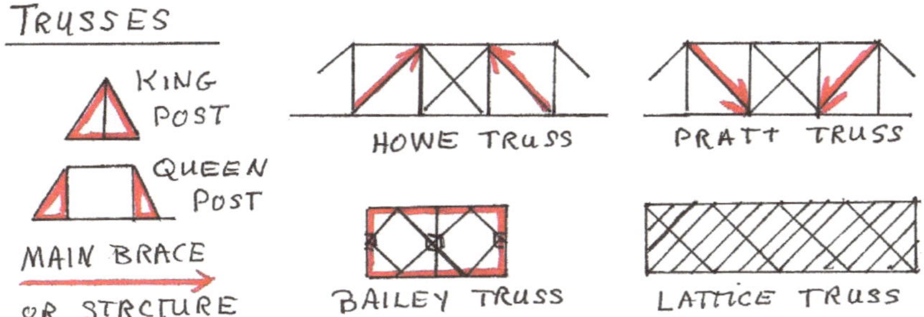

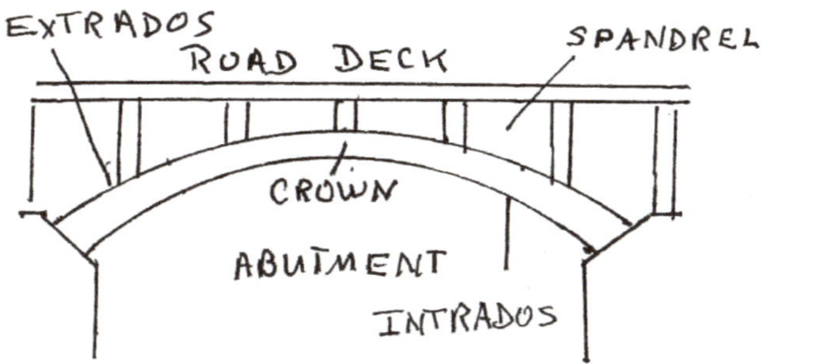

****References—Definitions and figures are an amalgam and compilation from my three primary sources of information.***

1. *Bridges—The Science and Art of the World's Most Inspiring Structures.* David Blockley, Oxford University Press. 2010
2. *Bridges: Three Thousand Years of Defying Nature.* David J. Brown, Firefly Books Ltd. 2005
3. *How to Read Bridges: A Crash Course in Engineering and Architecture.* Edward Denison and Ian Stuart, Rizzoli International Publications. 2012

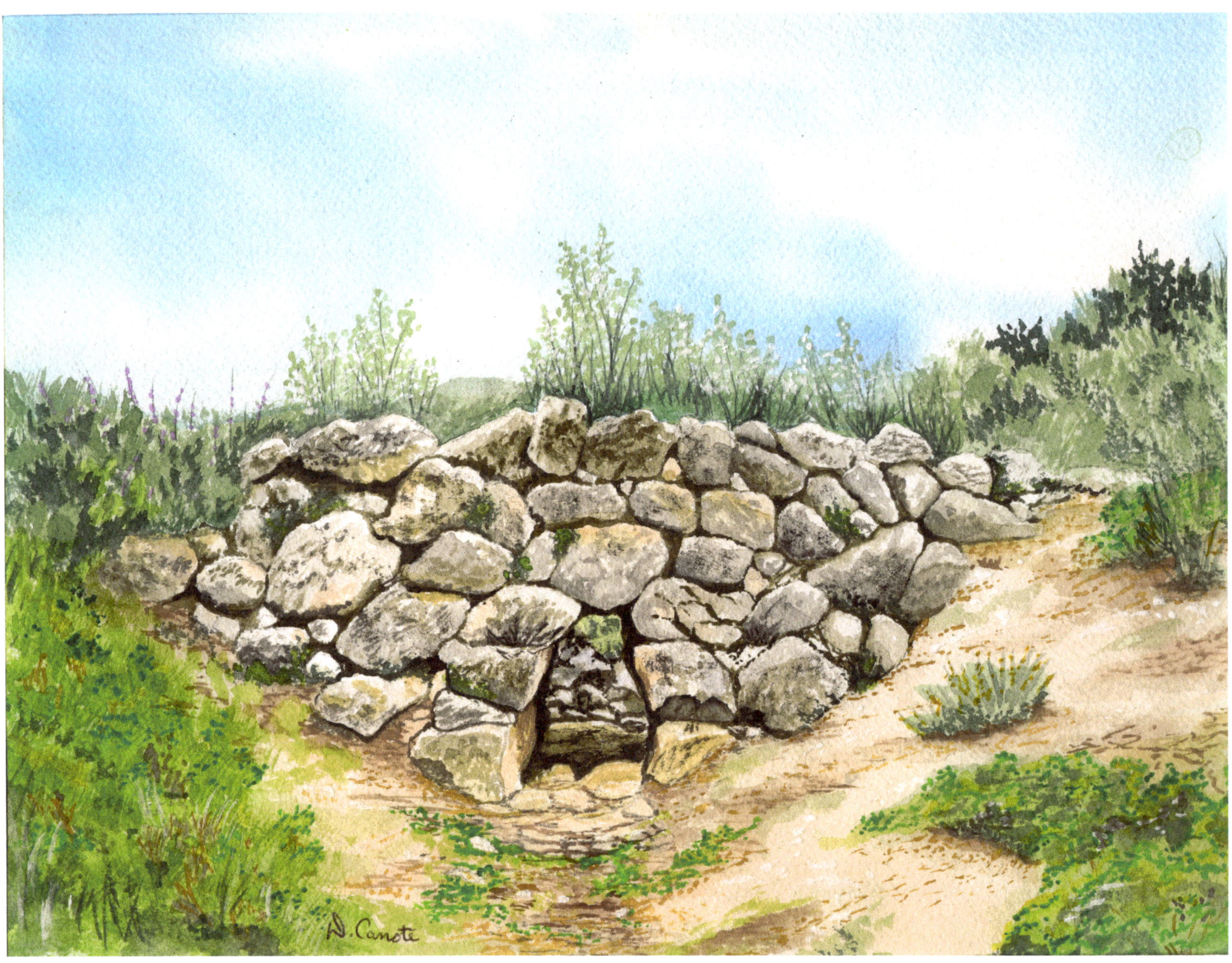
D. Canote

The Arkadiko and Other Ancient Bridges

I did a lot of reading about bridges, looking for the oldest technologies and the oldest still surviving bridge structures. Some of the oldest and simplest still in evidence are undoubtedly like one found in Somerset, England, called the Tarr Steps. Images can be found online if you are interested. The Tarr Steps bridge consists of flat rectangular slabs of stone a foot or two wide and a few feet long, their ends resting on stacks of similar stone slabs. A dozen or more of these sections join to cross the River Barle, a relatively shallow waterway comparable to many Ozark streams. Referred to as *clapper* bridges, each stack of supporting stone piers is buttressed by a stairstep of leaning stones that divert water between the piers and reduce the force of the water acting to dislodge the piers. There is no way to date such a bridge, and its first construction is relegated to the mists of prehistory.

Of the surviving ancient bridge examples, the Arkadiko Bridge is one of the oldest arch bridges still in existence and use, dating to the Bronze Age—3000 to 1200 B.C.E. This bridge and three other Mycenaean corbel arch bridges are part of a former network of roads designed to accommodate chariots between the fort of Tiryns and the town of Epidauros in the Peloponnese region of southern Greece. Archaeologists have determined the roadway across the bridge to be curbed, to guide the wheels of chariots.

When I saw a picture of this bridge, its rugged simplicity called to me to paint it. Built of limestone boulders and assembled without mortar, it is seventy-two feet long, eighteen feet wide, and thirteen feet high. While not as impressive as the larger, more modern examples of human engineering, the fact that it is still standing after over three thousand years should be a lesson to us all when we get a little too proud of ourselves. Simplicity and utility should be the hallmark of an enduring life.

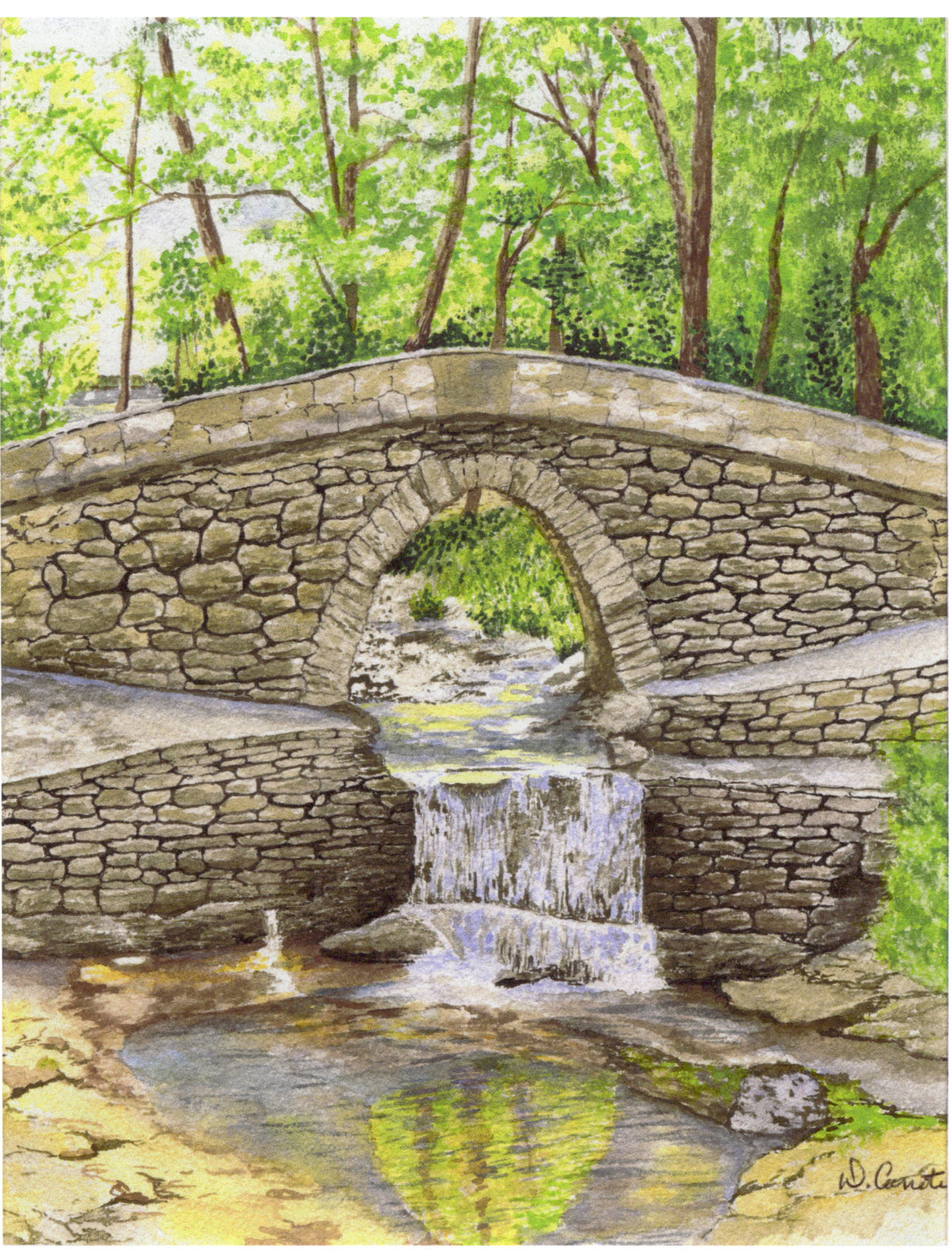

The Stone Bridge at Mountain View, Arkansas

For several years I traveled, sometimes alone and sometimes with other of my fellow herb growers, to Mountain View, Arkansas, to the spring and fall herb meetings at the Ozark Folk Center. Spring meetings featured a field trip to surrounding farms, parks and natural areas in search of wild and naturalized herbs having historical medicinal and culinary uses.

On one spring trip we hiked from the Folk Center itself down an adjacent creek, ending up at a nearby park. There the stream passed under a beautiful stone arch bridge that I was naturally compelled to photograph. I actually painted this bridge twice, the first a small five-by-seven inch which I sold to a couple who had a sentimental attachment to the site, having celebrated their nuptials at the bridge. Then, having embarked on the journey to write, I had to paint it again to include it in this journal.

This bridge is an example of a voussoir arch, featuring wedge-shaped stones in the arch and finished at the top by a capstone. I could find no specific historical reference to this bridge, but it is nearly identical to several others in the area constructed by the Civilian Conservation Corps (CCC) during the Works Project Administration (WPA) era. Like many such projects, this bridge has survived intact and beautifully, a testament to the talent and hard work of those who contributed so much to the infrastructure of our communities.

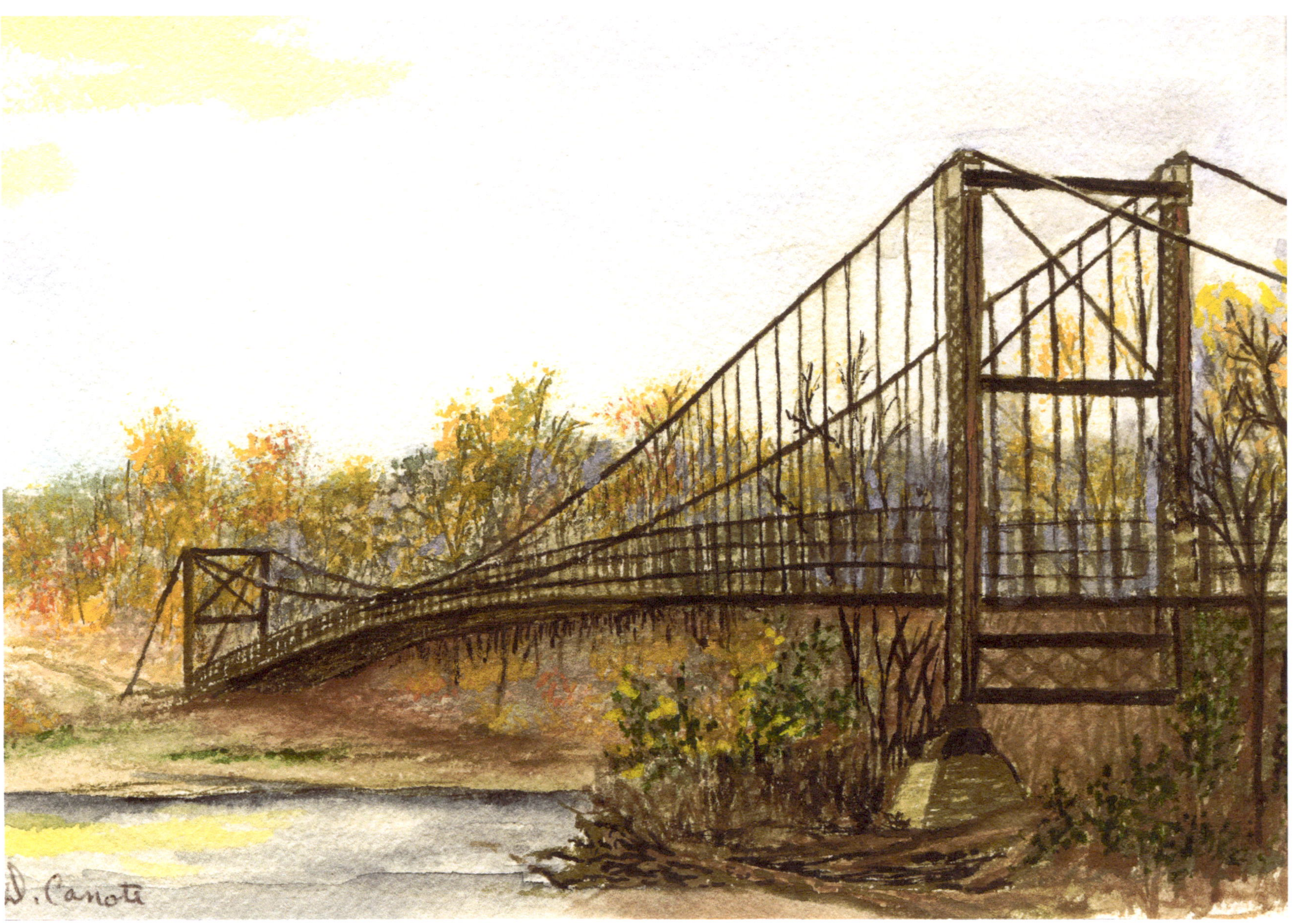
D. Canoti

The Swinging Bridges of Brumley

Just west of Brumley, Missouri, in Lake of the Ozarks State Park on Lake Road 42-18 lie two swinging bridges. These historic steel cable suspension bridges are located at the Mill Creek-Grand Glaize confluence. The larger of the two bridges, portrayed in my painting, is the four-hundred-foot Auglaize Bridge and spans Grand Glaize Creek, while the smaller one-hundred-foot steel suspension bridge spans Mill Creek. The bridges are at right angles to one another and one-thousand feet apart by roadway. While they can still be crossed (observing their weight limits), they are wooden decked. This is necessary for flexibility, but makes for a somewhat hair-raising drive across their span!

When I found a photo on Bridgehunter.com by James Baughn of this suspension bridge I immediately grasped its beauty, while at the same time I despaired at the challenge of painting its suspension wires! It was actually easier once I got started, but then I began researching the bridge and found my way down another rabbit hole, or perhaps it was "through the looking glass"?

This bridge, along with some thirty other suspension bridges, was designed and built by an engineer named Joseph Dice between 1836 and 1940. With only a fourth grade education, he became regionally well known as a consistently competent bridge builder. There is little or no documentation for his bridges, which indicates that they were built for local road districts. With no drawn plans or specifications, he relied solely on his memory and an intuition for the materials and design required. Most of Dice's bridges were financed by local 'subscriptions' and simply constructed using timber harvested from along the rivers and streams.

I recently learned a new word usage that applies to Joseph Dice's designs, as well as historic buildings. The term *vernacular architecture* refers to designs that are common to a place and time. His bridges were comparatively less costly to build, due to their economical design and use of local materials, and were "breathtakingly" light. The were adequate in strength for the traffic of the time but have fared poorly, so that only ten remain in place today.

Boeckmann Bridge

I think suspension bridges are among the most beautiful of man-made structures. They remind me of a spider's web, as from a distance their suspension members appear like fine strands, holding the bridge deck floating above the space it spans. Newer suspension bridges are popping up all over the country as white cable-stayed creations, lighted at night so they look like something out of an icy winterland fantasy.

Suspension bridges were probably among the first connections built across the deep crevasses in countries where terrain is so dissected as to prevent easy access from one side of a ravine to the other. Built by indigenous populations of native materials—vine, cane, hemp rope, and the like—such bridges are relatively light and flexible. Even though they have a fairly short life span due to natural processes of decay and deterioration, they can be cheaply rebuilt as long as the techniques to do so are retained in the memory of the community and passed along from generation to generation. For shorter spans over moderate depths, wood and metal suspension bridges were commonly built in areas where timber was plentiful and cheap.

The Boeckmann Bridge is a two-hundred-forty-foot long, fourteen-foot wide timber suspension bridge built by Joseph Dice in 1926. Named for Joseph Boeckmann, who donated the right-of-way for the bridge's construction, it is located near a public access to a favorite swimming spot on Big Tavern Creek, off Missouri Highway 52 southeast of Saint Elizabeth. It was rehabilitated in 1976 and replaced for traffic by a concrete bridge in 2002-2003. It is the only structure in Miller County which has been placed on the prestigious National Register of Historic Places.

I feel a particular affection for Tavern Creek, having spent an afternoon and night there with a fellow grad student, helping her on one of her collecting trips. We were both in Fisheries and Wildlife, and her research involved documenting the presence and distribution of two species of skulpin in Ozark streams. These ugly little bottom-dwelling fish have a great many more relatives in salt water than fresh water, so I had never before encountered them and was charmed by their ugliness.

But this particular trip was the quintessential graduate student experience, involving getting the truck stuck on the way to the camp site. Imagine two women struggling to get the truck out of the mud hole, which we finally did.

Once at the campsite clearing we encountered the incongruity of a huge overstuffed lounge chair beside a fire pit. How humorous! We set up our tent and proceeded to build a fire and prepare supper, consisting of typical grad student camp food featuring beans, hot dogs, sauerkraut, and onions, plus undoubtedly some beer (funny I can't remember much about that). I said, "My God, Nadine! We won't need to net the fish, we'll just gas them out of the stream!"

Well, we did actually find some skulpins . . . .

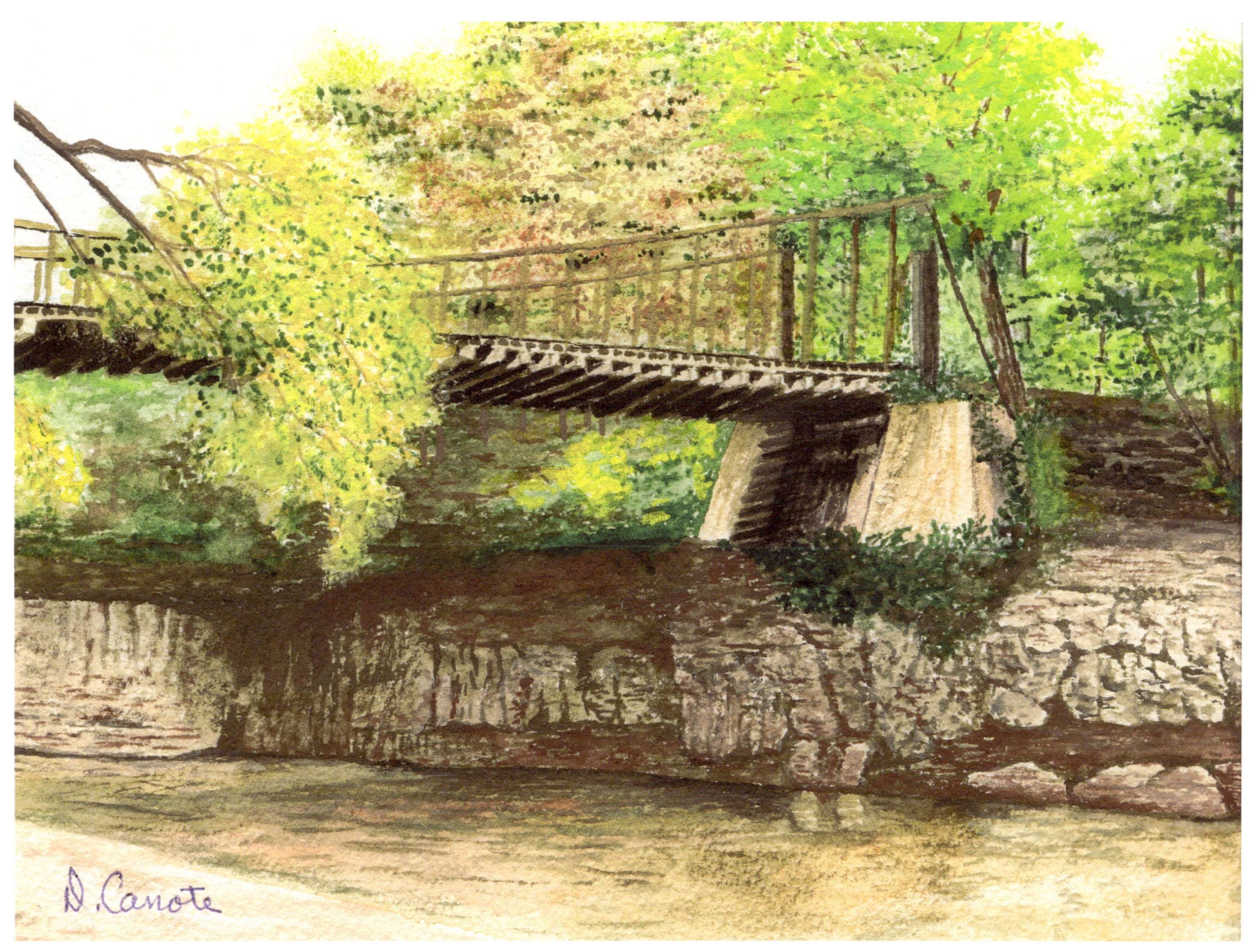
D. Canote

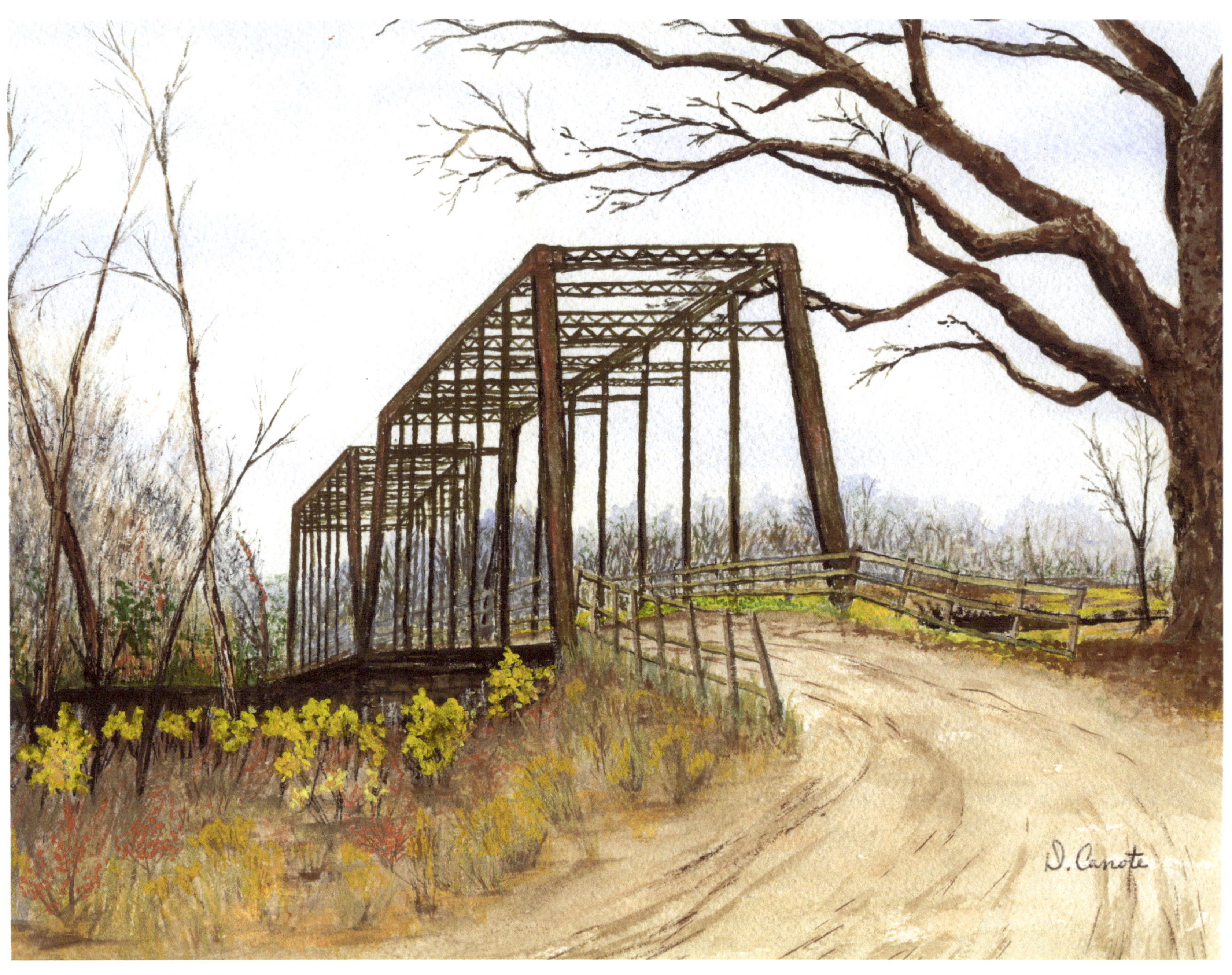
D. Canote

The Old Bedford Bridge

A black and white photo from the 1950s by Bill Plummer of this old truss bridge was posted on the Avalon Facebook page. Referred to as a through-truss bridge, it is typical of many of the old iron and steel bridges throughout Missouri and other central states. The first through-truss design, so called because one passes through the bridge structure across the bridge's deck, was made of iron and patented in 1841; by the 1880s and 1890s construction was transitioning to steel. Truss design was economical of materials and cost.

The Bedford Bridge was destroyed by a fallen elm in 1958, and was mostly swept away down the Grand River. While it existed, the bridge carried traffic from eastern Livingston County, Missouri and surrounding townships to the larger population center of Chillicothe. Traffic along this roadway likely also passed across the Jimtown Bridge south of Highway 36, also lost to history and the memory of all but a few really old folks. My Grandmother Fullerton once told me of a roadhouse situated near the Jimtown Bridge where highwaymen would lie in wait to accost travelers as they left the inn and passed across the floodplain bottoms of the Grand River before reaching Chillicothe.

The early bridges of this type were built on roads that carried what we would now call "farm to market" traffic. The roads themselves ranged from mud—or gravel if local taxes would support it—to asphalt, or nearer the towns, concrete roadways. Today, as these bridges are aging and reaching their life's end of usefulness, they are gradually being replaced by concrete and steel bridges of more modern but less interesting design. Still, there is something impressive about these old bridges, and they evoke a perhaps dubious nostalgia of a by-gone era, given that not everyone made it home safely.

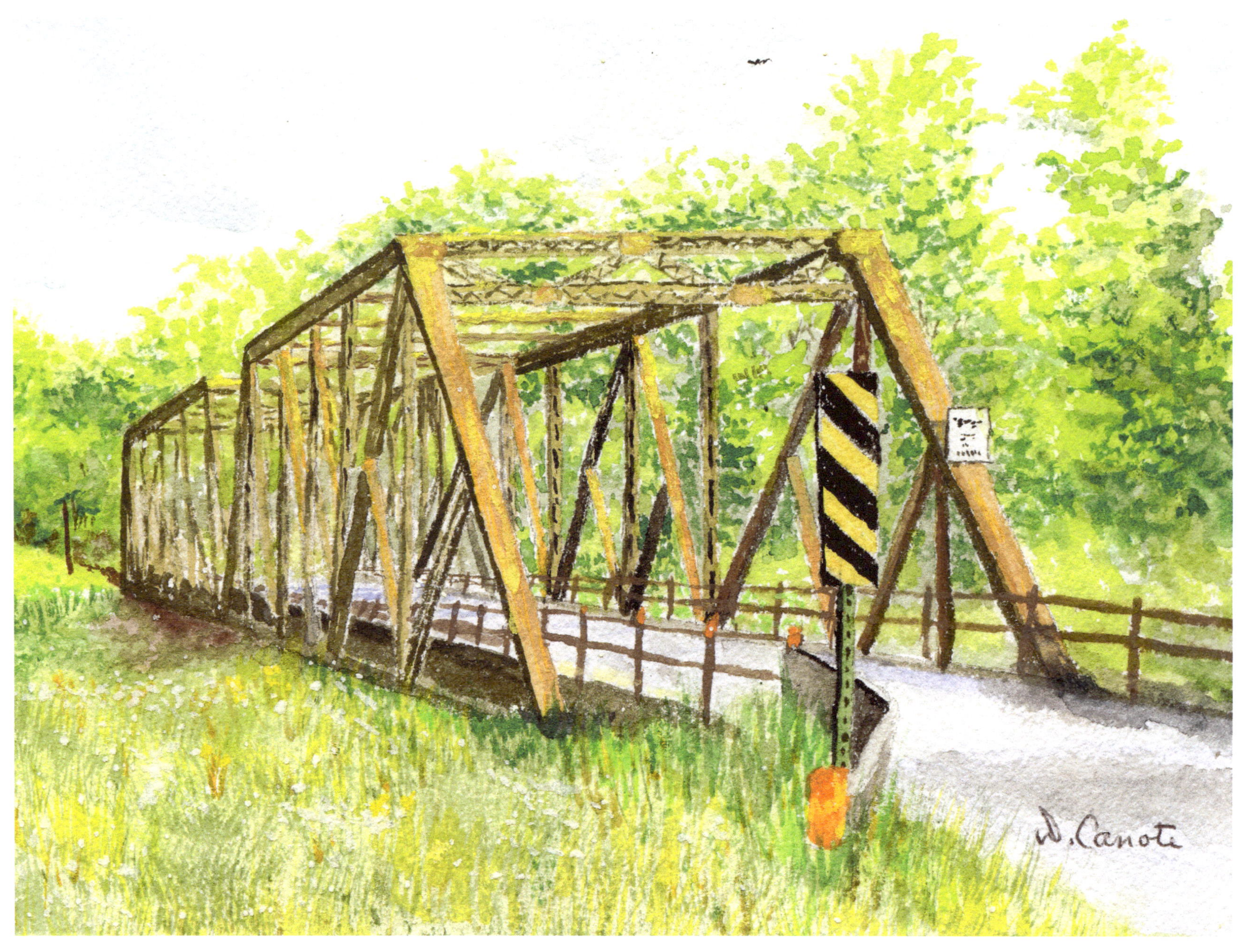

Charlie Dye Bridge

I ran across a photo of this bridge by Charles Robinson on Bridgehunter.com. I appreciated it immediately because of its proximity to Crowder State Park, where I attended both church and 4-H camp throughout my school years. Located on old Highway 6 in Grundy County, it spans the Thompson River, which flows south to the Grand River just north of Chillicothe, Missouri. You would not encounter it on a random drive, but I was intrigued by the story that accompanied it.

The Rock Island Railroad had a maintenance facility in Trenton beginning around 1900. Locomotives were overhauled at the roundhouse for Kansas City terminals, so this facility was an important source of jobs for the area. In the 1940s a bitter strike led to a serious conflict between strikers and scab workers who, following the Great Depression, were still hard pressed to find work.

The strike breakers walked several miles to the roundhouse, carrying their tool boxes. One strike-breaker named Hobbs, encountering a group of drunken union strike-breakers at the end of the bridge, pulled out a tool that might be mistaken for a pistol and put it in his pocket. The drunken thugs harassed him, but seeing his hand in his pocket with the ominous bulge, backed away and let him pass. The next scab to cross the bridge, however, did not fare so well and was beaten to death.

The politics of the time favored the strikers, and local authorities were not inclined to prosecute. However, the Rock Island executives were far from pleased. They settled the strike but moved the overhaul base to Kansas City, closing the roundhouse. Losing a major employer, the city experienced a decline in population growth which continues today.

Charlie Dye Bridge is another example of the ubiquitous two-span through-truss bridges so common throughout the Midwest. Now closed to through traffic due to the condition of its deck and structure, it is still compellingly dignified and to me, beautiful and sad in its rust and age.

Springfield Des Arc Bridge

Looking for examples of certain types of bridges was frustrating, and sometimes I looked outside of Missouri for the examples I needed. Arkansas, whose physical geography, soil, and road system is similar to Missouri, also provided some very nice bridge specimens. This bridge is actually a hybrid between an arch bridge and a suspension bridge, and its unique structure deserves some explanation.

North of Conway, Arkansas, in Faulkner County, the Springfield Des Arc Bridge was constructed by King Bridge Manufactory and Iron Works in 1874. Spanning the north branch of Cadron Creek, it is the oldest remaining highway bridge in Arkansas, as well as the only remaining cast-iron and wrought-iron bowstring arch bridge in the state. Although listed as a pony truss bridge by one reference, the arches are not trusses but tubular iron. A pony truss bridge is typically open at the top, while the name "bow-string" (also known as a bow-string girder) has an arch rib on each side of the roadway deck and one tie beam on each arch. Vertical ties connected to the arches support the deck from above. This bridge has wooden beams and flooring on the deck.

With construction similar to a traditional re-curve bow, the tips of this arch are tied together at the bottom by its connection to the deck. The load of the deck (thrust) is transferred as tension to the arch. Such structures can be prefabricated off site and floated, hauled or lifted into place. Since they are not tied into the site itself, they require less robust foundations and can be placed atop elevated piers or in areas of unstable soil.

Construction and design of this bridge is non-redundant, which means that if one of the two tie girders fail, the whole structure will collapse without anything to work as safety. Tied arch bridges are more expensive to build compared to the other types of bridges of the same length, and old ones like this are subject to failure due to poor welding at the joints. Sort of like some of us old folks, eh?

A photo by Wayne Kizziar was inspiration for this painting.

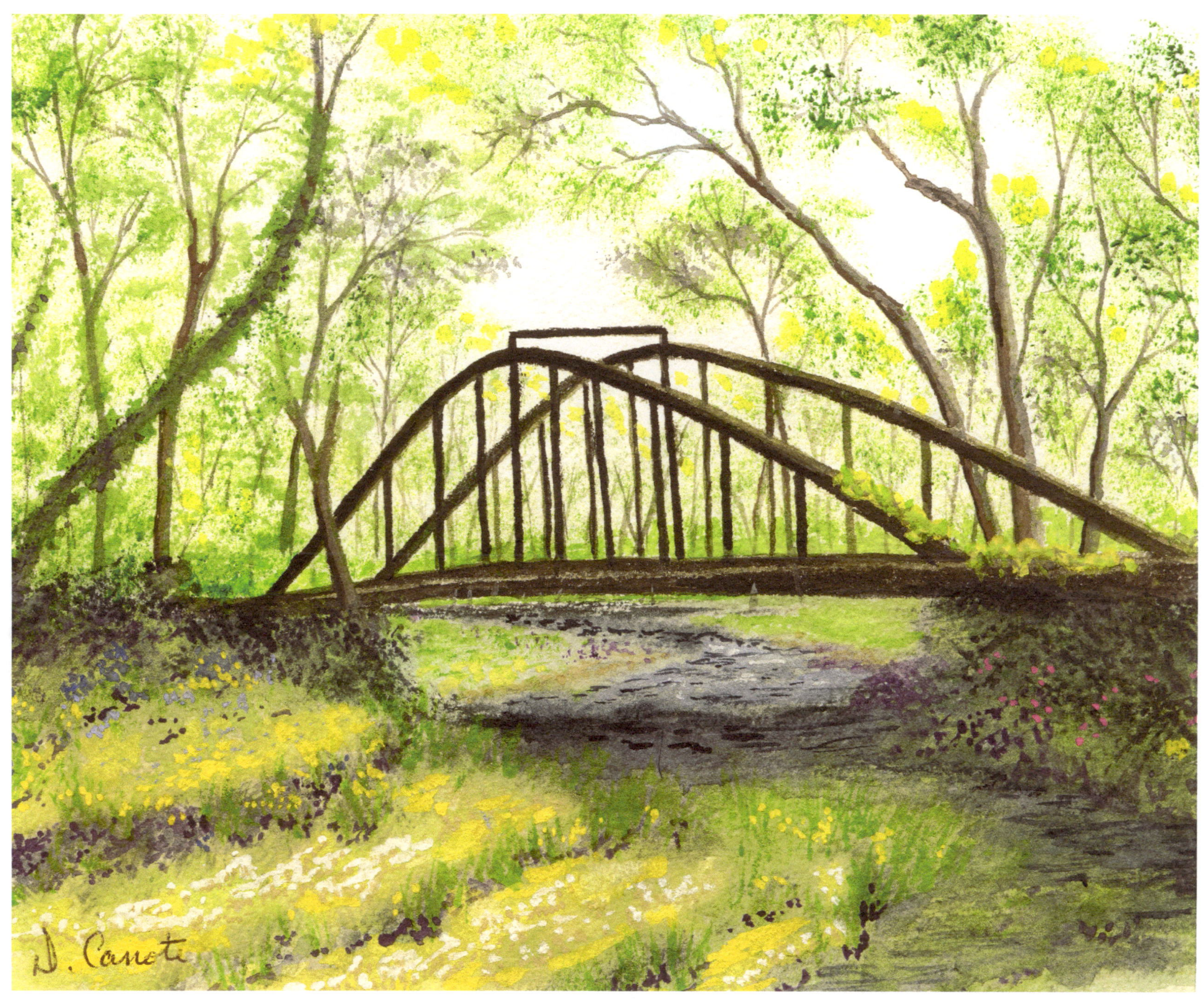
D. Canoti

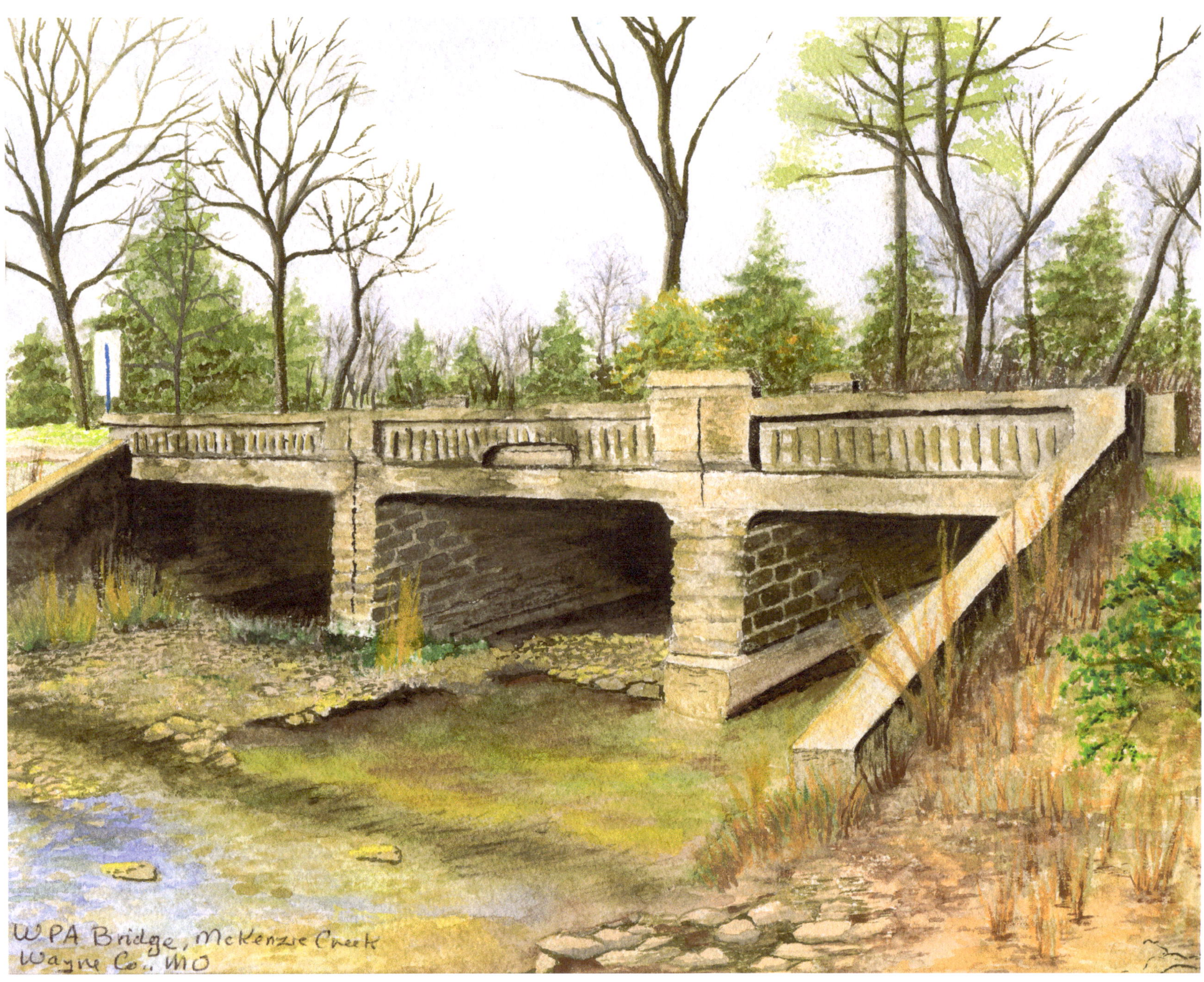
W.P.A Bridge, McKenzie Creek
Wayne Co., MO

McKenzie Creek Bridge

This bridge over McKenzie Creek is located approximately 1.4 miles west of Greenville on Route CC in Wayne County. This is a three-span concrete-slab bridge with stone abutments and piers. No date was given for its construction but it was probably a WPA or CCC project. I once flippantly remarked, upon hearing my mother make reference to the WPA, "We Piddle Around," having no doubt heard that said while eavesdropping on another conversation. She was instantly inflamed, informing me that I should never, *ever* say that again in her hearing, and that the WPA was what enabled a lot of families, including my own, to survive who would otherwise had a very difficult time during the Great Depression of the 1930s and 1940s.

Most of the state's population in those years was rural and farmers suffered greatly. Families had little money to spare and had to live off what they could grow on their land. A devastating drought in the early thirties greatly impacted farmers in the western portion of the state, leading to migrations to other states or to cities in search of work. Unemployment was high and once people lost their jobs, they soon lost their homes.

My parents both passed long before I knew enough to ask questions about their early married lives. I do know that my dad's father had a stud farm, providing various kinds of livestock for breeding purposes, and that they also grew field crops and vegetables for the family's table. My father was also a welder, and when work was scarce or unavailable at the end of World War II (mid-1940s), our family—Mom, Dad and two brothers—moved to Chicago where he welded for Link Belt and worked as a guard for Pinkerton at some of the big warehouses. My mother took in ironing, and also worked in a grocery warehouse where she recalled (shuddering) large tarantulas crawling out of the bunches of bananas from countries south of the United States.

Now, every time I drive across one of these old concrete bridges, with chips missing and concrete breaking apart, I think about my mother and her comment. These old bridges are a heritage that gets little recognition or appreciation. There are so many throughout the country that you can hardly drive any distance through rural Missouri without crossing one. I could find very little information about their history or construction. They are all definitely older than I am, but only by a few years, so I value what they represent and cherish their service.

This painting is in homage to James Baughn's lovely photo of the bridge that tripped a creative impulse in me.

Newman Bridge

First I'll tell you a little bit about the bridge and then I'll tell you about another rabbit hole I fell into trying to find something noteworthy to say about it.

This concrete girder bridge over the West Fork of Tebo Creek on County Road NE 500 in Henry County was built in 1917 by the Canton (Ohio) Bridge Company, from which the photo came. Bridge Hunter reports that it was replaced in 1998, but doesn't specify whether the photo is of the old or the new bridge.

Failing to find any more about the bridge, I searched afield for some other tidbit about the county itself. Henry County lies approximately half way between Kansas City and Springfield on the west side of Missouri. About 80 percent of the county is forested and moderately hilly, much of it bordering public lands surrounding Truman Reservoir. The economy is mainly agricultural and the city of Clinton is the county seat. Finding not much to say about that, I wondered if the county produced any persons of note.

It did, and now about the rabbit hole . . .

I never formally studied art, though I am moderately acquainted with the more well known classical and modern painters. However, I had never heard of Harry Louis Freund. Louis was born in Clinton, September 16, 1905. Educated at the University of Missouri in Columbia and Washington University in Saint Louis, he then traveled to Paris for further study. Returning to the United States he began winning commissions from the Works Project Administration to paint murals in such places as Arkansas, Florida, Kansas, Oklahoma, Texas, and Missouri. It was during this period that he designed the Missouri mural for the 1933 Chicago World's Fair.

You would have to search the web to appreciate the diversity of his work. His painting style seems to me quite variable, his subjects ranging from mural landscapes to urban scenes, to dance halls, even a bit of portraiture. Some murals are similar in style to Thomas Hart Benton, and can still be seen on walls of U.S. Post Offices and other public buildings. In 1936 he was hired as artist-in-residence at Hendrix College in Conway, Arkansas. It was about this time that he met his wife, Elsie.

Elsie Marie Bates was best known as a studio art jeweler, watercolorist, and textile artist. She was of Irish-Cherokee heritage, born in Taney county in 1912, near the town of Mincey, Missouri, just four miles north of the Arkansas border. Her education was perhaps less prestigious than Freund's, but after a year of teaching she was able to attend the Kansas City Art Institute for one year. Then she returned to Branson and opened a gift shop selling her own creations of walnut jewelery and other crafts. Accepted in 1953 into the National Watercolor Society, she also developed her own tie-dye technique for watercolor. Following a course in ceramics at the Wichita Art Association in Kansas, she established her own jewelery business, for which she is best known. She developed unique designs in combinations of clay, glass, and silver which she sold through a New York City craft outlet, America House.

Elsie and Louis married in 1939, moving to Florida in 1949 where Louis taught at Stetson University. Upon his retirement in 1967 they returned to Eureka Springs, Arkansas where they lived for the remainder of their lives.

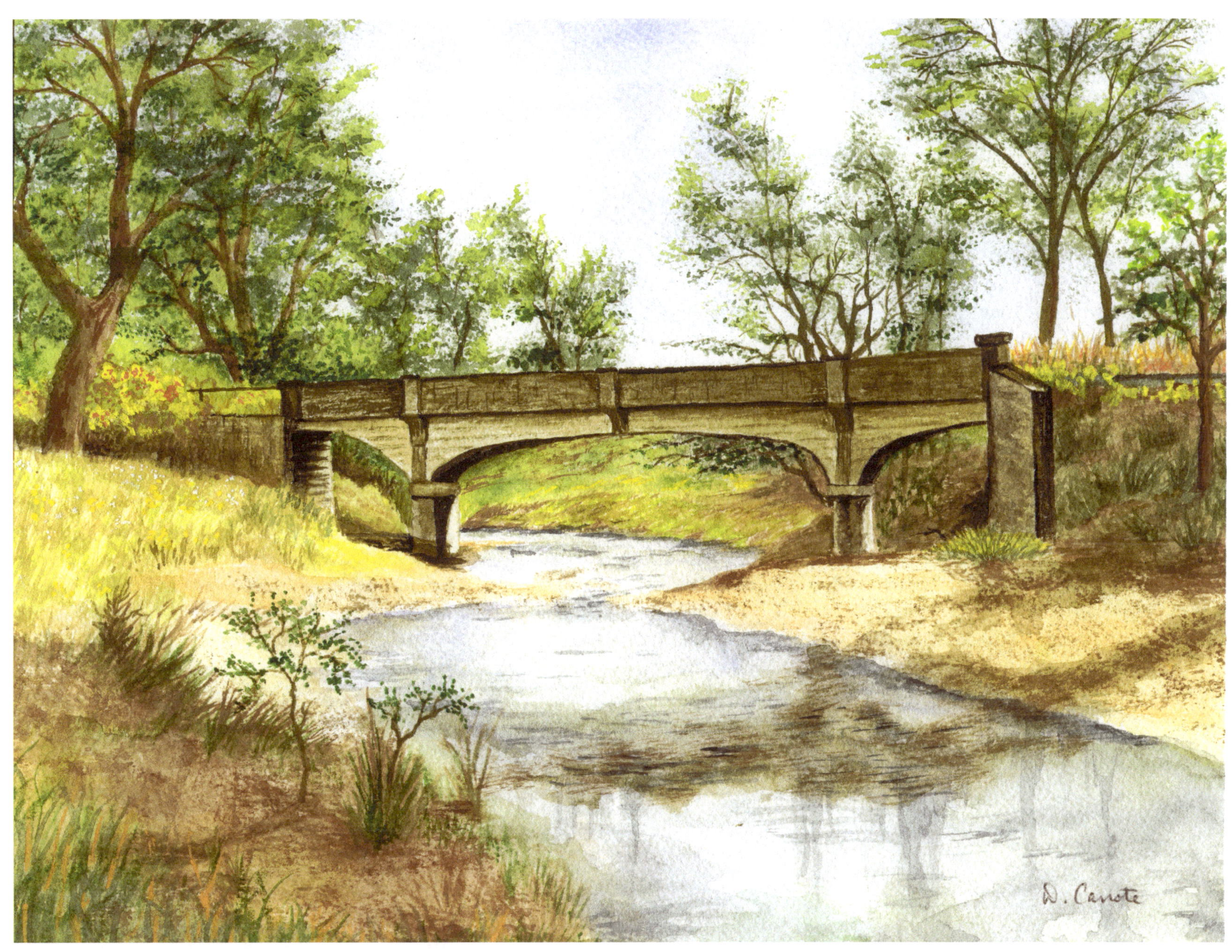

Graham's Mill Covered Bridge

When I was researching covered bridges in Missouri I happened to find a reference to Graham's Mill and the bridge named for that site. My painting was done from an old postcard, the only photo archive available. It was located in Livingston County, about four miles northwest of the county seat of Chillicothe. At one time there was a ferry located there, and the northwest part of Livingston County, which now comprises the townships of Jackson and Sampsel, was one of the most densely settled parts of the county. This ferry soon became a very important link for the people of this part of the county traveling to and from Chillicothe.

The traffic became so heavy that in 1866 and 1867 a bridge was built across Grand River at this location. There is some confusion about this point, because what was historically called Grand River is now referred to as the Thompson River, which is a branch of the Grand. The bridge was constructed of native white oak timbers that were cut and shaped in the forests growing nearby.

James Graham in 1867 chose a site near this ferry and bridge for the erection of a mill, known since as Graham's Mill. The fact that this site was favorable for the construction of a dam (to furnish the power for day to day operation) added to its importance as a mill site. Not only did the people of Livingston County use this bridge, but many of the residents of the counties north and west chose this route to get their produce and merchandise to and from Chillicothe, the shipping point on the Hannibal and Saint Joseph Railroad.

Information provided here was taken from one article in a series on the history of mills of Livingston County. Written by George W. Somerville of Chillicothe, former president of the Grand River Historical Society and Museum, the article provides additional information and insight into earlier times.

The mill was first operated by James Graham and later by his brother, Oliver. Oliver Graham possessed a striking appearance, with whiskers so long they were rolled into a knot and secured with a hairpin to prevent entanglement with the revolving machinery. He was also a somewhat obsessive man with a compulsion for keeping the mill clean. It seems that one day a farmer, who was there to have his grist ground, spit his chewing tobacco onto the floor. Without comment, Mr. Graham dragged the farmers sack of meal through the spittle, wiping the floor clean.

The Grand River was then, and still is, a favored fishing spot, and the old covered bridge was a venue for picnics and dances. Originally a stone mill, the grindstone was replaced by a roller mill around 1890, and continued to operate until 1909 or 1910. This old covered bridge stood for seventy seven years and on May 2, 1944 was destroyed by a flood.

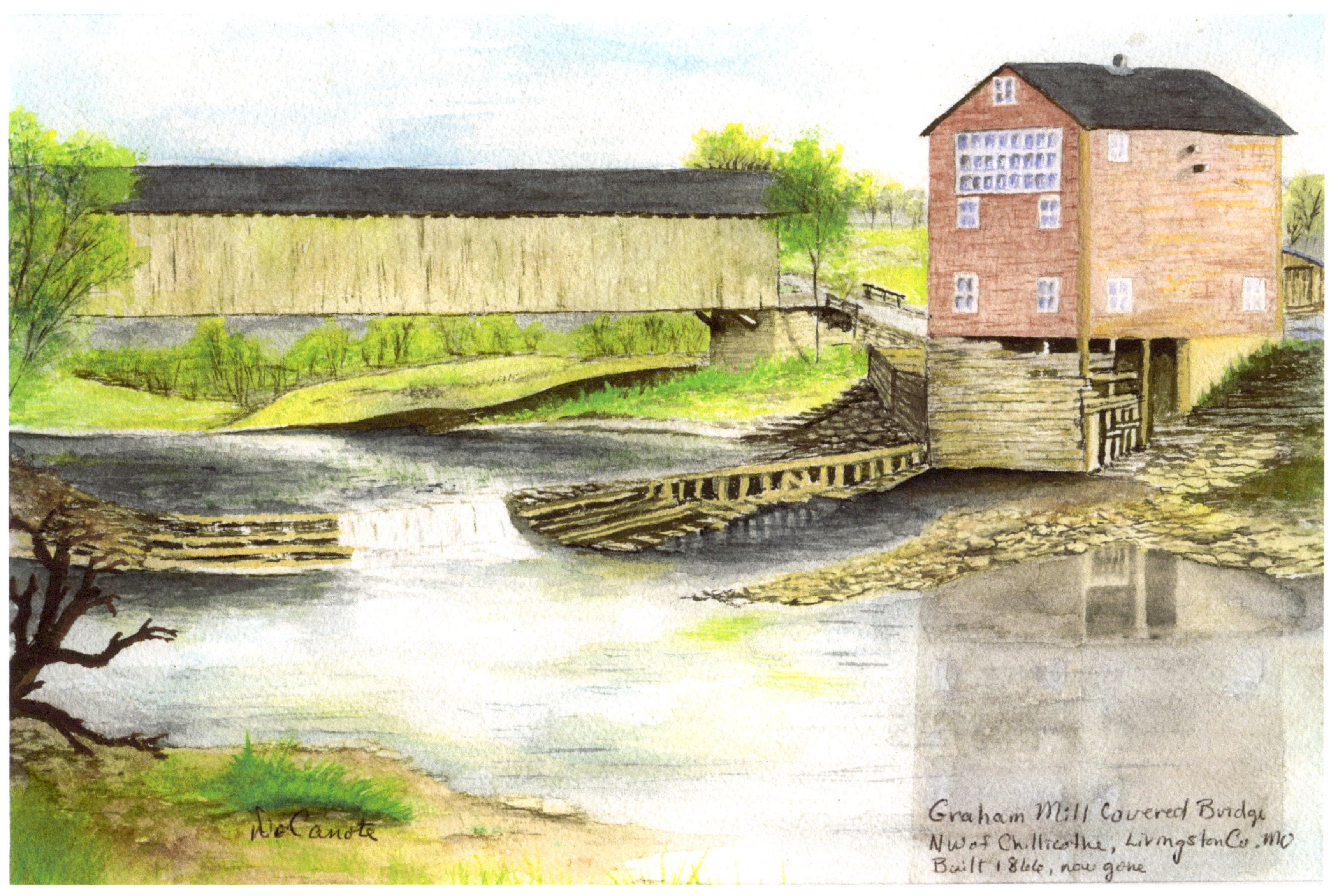
DeCamote
Graham Mill Covered Bridge
NW of Chillicothe, Livingston Co. MO
Built 1866, now gone

Acknowledgments

Many thanks to:

Yolanda Ciolli, my brilliant editor and publisher whose patient guidance led me through this first effort, and who became another wonderful friend.

The Grand River Historical Society and the Miller County Historical Society for granting the use of photos from their archives as subjects for some of my paintings.

All the hard-working photographers whose photos of bridges and buildings called me to paint them.

My spiritual sisters of the Columbia Art Group who contribute their ideas, support, and inspiration in our weekly gatherings.

About the Artist

Born in Chicago in 1946, Dorothy Catherine Canote proudly claims her baby boomer status. She grew up in Avalon, Missouri.

Dorothy earned her Bachelor of Science in Biology from Missouri Valley College before beginning her teaching career in 1968. She returned to academia in 1980 and earned a Masters degree in Agronomy from the University of Missouri–Columbia in 1983, followed by post graduate studies at MU in Fisheries and Wildlife.

In 1997, Dorothy began a ten year stint teaching science at Hickman High School in Columbia. Now retired, Dorothy grows produce, herbs, and flowers and is a member of the Columbia Farmers Market. She has also rediscovered her love for art and is a watercolor painter. This is her first book.

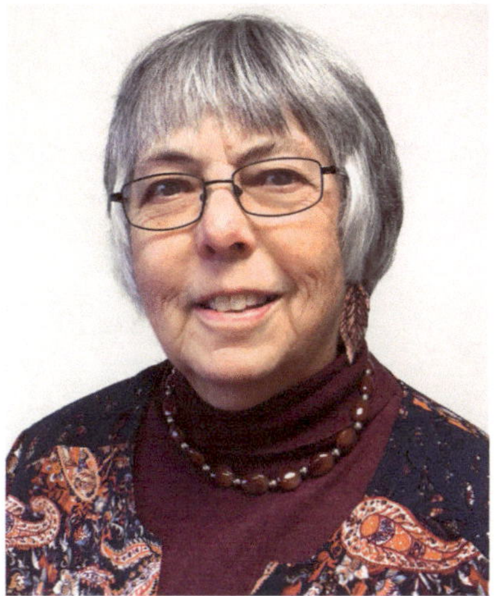

www.ingramcontent.com/pod-product-compliance
Lightning Source LLC
LaVergne TN
LVHW072331100826
845154LV00010B/154